Your Pain is Not in Vain

©Copyright 2023- Jennifer Whitaker

All rights reserved. This book may not be copied or reprinted for commercial gain or profit. The use of short quotations or occasional page copying for personal, or group study is permitted and encouraged. Permission will be granted upon request.

THE HOLY BIBLE, NEW INTERNATIONAL VERSION®, NIV® Copyright © 1973, 1978, 1984, 2011 by Biblica, Inc.® Used by permission. All rights reserved worldwide.

Your Pain is Not in Vain

Jennifer Whitaker

CONTENTS

Introduction

Chapter 1: Jesus, the Way..............................7

Chapter 2: Lost..25

Chapter 3: The Crossroad............................55

Chapter 4: Glorious.....................................77

Chapter 5: Smash the Rearview....................83

Chapter 6: Accepted....................................95

Chapter 7: Trusting the Father....................105

Chapter 8: Kairos-An Appointed Time..........119

Chapter 9: Get Ready to Shift.....................129

Chapter 10: Don't Miss Your Moment..........139

Chapter 11: Supernatural Hand of God........149

Chapter 12: Way Maker..............................155

Chapter 13: Another Shift..........................163

Chapter 14: He is the Door.........................177

Chapter 15: Unexpected Surprises..............185

Chapter 16: Fulfillment..............................199

Introduction

Well, here it is, Lord! I have begun to put the words together to explain the radical transformation that has taken place in my life, where the old passed away and the new began. Looking back on it, I think to myself, "Only the grace and mercy of God have kept me alive and even kept me sane." Believing that the God of this universe loves you and me so much to come and rescue us from the dark grips of Satan's hand is still mind-blowing. What a great love!

My hope is that the Holy Spirit ministers to you through reading this book and reveals the Lord's awesome plans and purposes for your life. There are no limits on the Lord, and He wants to use you in a mighty and powerful way in this end-time harvest! I pray my testimony of how the Lord rescued me from gross darkness and restored my life to the point that I feel as though I am dreaming now encourages your heart! Psalm 126:1 says, "When the Lord restored the fortunes of Zion, we were like those who dreamed." When you live in sin for so long, you become used to chaos, but when you invite the Prince of Peace into your life, it is a peace that surpasses ALL understanding.

As you see on the cover of this book, there are beautiful butterflies. The conversion process from a caterpillar to a butterfly is called "metamorphosis." Romans 12:2 says, "Do not conform to the pattern of this world but be transformed by the renewing of your mind. Then you will be able to test and approve what God's will is-His good, pleasing, and perfect will." That Word "transform" would be correctly translated from the original Greek as "metamorphoo," which is where we get the word "metamorphosis." Metamorphosis is the changing of one thing into something more significant. It is like the incorruptible seed (Word) and how it completely changes us into a brand-new person (into His image).

A caterpillar is not the most beautiful of creatures; it crawls on the ground until it is wrapped into what seems like a "temporary prison." This is what we call a cocoon or chrysalis. You may be in a hidden place today, but you must know that the Lord works in you as you hide in Him.

Caterpillars eat non-stop and can double their size in just a day. They grow so much that they continually shed their skin. It is similar to how parts of us must shed off as we grow in the Lord. It is like being born again, and as we consume the Word, shedding the old ways, we become brand new. We are being transformed. As we continue to consume the Word, we go through a metamorphosis. This process allows us to break out of old, carnal thought patterns, allowing us to fly!

I dedicate this book to my Lord Jesus, my mother in the faith, my mentor, and my best friend, Laura Crocker. Your yes to Jesus and your laid-down life of love have impacted my life forever, and I am eternally grateful. Thank you for loving me so well!

Thank you to every minister that has poured into my life since first surrendering to Christ! There are too many to list all those who have impacted my life, but I am so grateful. I know I would not be where I am today had it not been for those that have discipled me along the way. Discipleship matters!

When I first surrendered to Christ in 2013, New Life Church in Farmville, Virginia, welcomed me with open arms. Pastors Bill and Jenny McIntosh, Pastor Betty, Pastors David and Amanda Malcolm just to name a few truly helped disciple me in my beginning steps with the Lord. Thank you all so very much!

To the Whichard family of Reach City Church in my hometown of Chesterfield, Virginia, thank you for praying for me and championing me in my calling. I am so thankful God led me to your family. You all have deeply impacted my life.

To Pastor Parsley and the Parsley family at World Harvest Church and Valor Christian College, thank you for your yes to the call and for being a voice of Truth in this generation. I am forever marked by my time under your ministry.

To the ministry of Christ for all Nations, Evangelist Daniel Kolenda, Evangelist Levi Lutz, and all the leadership in this soul-winning ministry, thank you for entrusting a generation of Holy Spirit Evangelists with the torch. I honor you! May we serve this generation well!

1.

Jesus, the Way

This is the story: His-story of how the Lord rocked my life with His magnificent power. The power of God that is readily available to us as Christians. As a kid, I rode a school bus to church, where a young lady a few houses down from us invited me. I remember how I felt so secure and safe when we were in that tabernacle. A comfort came upon me: the Presence of Almighty God. I repented and received Jesus into my heart, and I remember so well how I loved singing, "This little light of mine."

Things began to shift at home after I finally talked my parents into attending church. There was a sense of peace and unity that we did not have before. After receiving Christ into my heart, it was as if I knew even then that Jesus was a friend that sticks closer than a brother. That lasted maybe a year and a half, and then things at home became chaotic again.

I did not grow up in a Christian environment, although my parents believed in God. There is a dramatic difference between believing there is a God and having a genuine encounter with Him. This is true transformation when you allow Him to change you from the inside out. Besides, the demons even believe in God.

It is not enough to merely believe and go to church, doing the same things you did before you were "saved." True Christianity is a heart conversion, where He replaces the hard heart with a heart of flesh, a heart sensitive to the Holy Spirit (Ezekiel 36:26). Romans 10:9-10 says, "If you declare with your mouth, 'Jesus is Lord,' and believe in your heart that

God raised him from the dead, you will be saved. For it is with your heart that you believe and are justified, and it is with your mouth that you profess your faith and are saved."

Jesus must be Lord of ALL of our life, or He is not Lord at all! Many people know Him to be Savior, but Lordship is another matter. Jesus died so that we could be saved from sin, which brings death spiritually and separation from God. Conversely, since we are free from sin, we can make Him Lord over every area of our life. This is true freedom, where we become like children, being willing and obedient to trust Him in ALL things.

Each of us is an eternal being and will one day spend eternity in one of two places: Heaven or hell. The choice is ours to receive this gift of salvation or to deny the Lamb of God's sacrifice, who died in our stead. We have been co-crucified with Him. Every sin, everything we have thought or done against the will of the Father, was nailed to that cross. Not only has our sin been nailed to the cross, but our sinful nature as well. We need to believe in the finished work of the cross.

Sadly, much of the American church does not even believe in hell, which is astonishing, mainly since the Lord spoke of hell more in the Bible than He referenced Heaven. I think that is because He is unwilling that any perish and that all come to repentance (2 Peter 3:9). He cries out, "I've already paid the price; IT IS FINISHED, choose LIFE!"

In the beginning stages of life, I never entirely understood that if God was good, why do good people go through terrible things? We all have had our questions. The bottom line is that we are born into a fallen world due to the fall of the first Adam, but Jesus came as the second Adam and redeemed us from the curse of the law, Hallelujah!

In the New Testament, Galatians 3:13 says, "Christ redeemed us from the curse of the law by becoming a curse for us, for it is written: Cursed is everyone who is hung on a pole." Deuteronomy 21:22-23 teaches that a divine curse was placed on a hanged person. "If someone guilty of a capital offense is put to death, and their body is exposed on a pole, you must not leave the body hanging on the pole overnight. Be sure to bury it that same day because anyone who is hung on a pole is under God's curse. You must not desecrate the land the Lord your God is giving you as an inheritance." Jesus died a criminal's death so that we could be free from the chains of sin. The separation that sin causes between God and man has been intersected in Him. The spotless lamb of God came down from Heaven's Glory to open access to the Father to all who will believe in Him.

What I have written on these pages is not meant to dishonor my parents. Everything I am sharing is a testament to God's mercy, love, and grace that turned my course of direction. I honor my parents and am thankful for the blood of Jesus that has redeemed our bloodline. My mother and father loved me and did their best with what they had. When we have not received the love and healing of God, it is hard to love others properly.

The beauty of being a child of God is that we become new creatures in Christ, and the old has passed away (2nd Corinthians 5:17). It is incredible to me that when we allow God to shape and form us, as He is the potter and we are the clay, what marvelous work He can do! To think He could turn the mess that I was into a message makes me tear up in gratitude. He is a great God and can turn your worst memory into an avenue of victory for you.

The older I get, the more I realize how the enemy, or satan, tries to come at a child's identity hard so that if they can perceive themselves in a skewed way, they will not accomplish much for God. As a man thinks in his heart, so is he (Proverbs 23:7). If the enemy can infiltrate your mind with harmful thoughts about yourself, he can, in that attempt, derail your destiny. As a child of God, if we knew the power and authority we possess by the shed blood of Jesus Christ, we would take dominion in regions for the Glory of God. Satan in Hebrew means "accuser" which is just what he is, a liar full of accusations against every child of God. Believe the Word and the Father's affirmation over you.

Many Christians live beneath what we have access to in the Spirit realm. Ephesians 2:6 says we are seated with Christ in heavenly places, and we can be conduits to bring Heaven unto Earth. We can speak His Word into situations and call those things not as if they were (Romans 4:17). This is faith, and it is the currency of Heaven!

Sadly, I see many who are afraid to take a risk, and they play it safe when the Christian walk is meant to be an exciting adventure. God has a perfect plan, but many settle for that: a good plan, not God's plan.

When you think of the horrible sacrificial death that Jesus paid and the extreme measures He took, don't you believe that we would be doing ourselves and Him an injustice if we did not go all out in our pursuit of Him and His purposes? We are called to lay down our lives, but sadly many want to go their way. They go to church on Sunday and live in the routine of religion. I get it! In my walk with God, I got to a place where I was going through the motions, but there was no faith in action. Hebrews 11:6 says, "And without faith, it is impossible to please God, because anyone who comes to him must believe that he exists and that he rewards those who earnestly seek him."

My endeavors in authoring this book and why the Lord intended for me to write it is to bring much hope to those broken down by life and the heartache it can bring. We all go through trials and tribulations on this Earth, but we all have a choice to move beyond our experiences and choose to move forward into purpose. Having a perspective that this life is not our home and that we are just pilgrims passing through helps us when things do not go as we had hoped. Even so, the Lord is sovereign overall. Thank God our hope is in Christ, the chief cornerstone, and not in the shifting and shakings of this world.

No matter what we go through, we must not allow the victim mentality of "woe is me" to keep us in stagnation. We have all been through less-than-perfect situations in our lifetime, but do not let a circumstance keep you in defeat. Hope deferred makes the heart sick (Proverbs 13:12). If you have been suffering from a broken heart, I pray that as you read this book, the healing balm of Gilead will heal your tattered soul and heart.

The Lord Jesus Christ is the well that will never run dry. The Word says He is living water and desires to refresh you, bringing life to your entire being if you allow Him. The Lord has given us all free will. Without a choice, it would not be love on our end. Love is a choice. He is a good Father, and when He created us, His purpose was to be in a relationship with us. Union with Him was the ultimate goal. He desired a family, so He made man. Hell was created for Satan and his demons. It was never a place where the Father intended for His creation to spend eternity. Deuteronomy 30:19 says, "This day I call the heavens and the Earth as witnesses against you that I have set before you life and death, blessings, and curses. Now choose life so that you and your children may live." Our lives are choice-driven and succeeding to consequences.

I think about when I first got out of jail; at times, I would get very frustrated with myself because it seemed like it took so many steps to get my license back, complete alcohol and drug programs, gain the trust back from loved ones, and gain back some dignity. It can be a process. Do not think that after many wrong choices you have made along the way, one day, you will decide to change course and make the right choices, and everything will change instantly. It did not take you a day to get into a mess, and it certainly will not take a day to get out of it.

It takes patience with God and yourself to redeem what has been lost, but trust that He is faithful to walk with you every step if you let Him. Although Jesus has redeemed us with His blood, all that was lost does not come handed on a silver platter immediately. We live in an instant "microwave" society and tend to want things fast and quick, but God is much more concerned with changing your heart and inner man than changing the circumstances around you. Otherwise, you may end up on that hard road again if you do not allow Him to change you internally. He wants to build your inner fortitude to sustain what He wants to do in your life.

I will share some of my testimony as the Holy Spirit leads and some learning experiences or hard truths that I have learned along the way. I pray that the lost, the broken, the outcast, the one who feels they have gone too far, might read this book and know that all is not lost. That through Christ Jesus, He can give you beauty for ashes. But some things need to be burnt up and purified to get ashes.

Jesus is not looking to come to do some superficial work on the outside of you. Jesus wants to tear down the old and completely rebuild, with Him being the firm foundation. He wants to come in and uproot your rejection from the womb. He wants to love the hate right from your heart towards the person who molested you as a kid. He desires to reach down into your heart and wants you to be vulnerable enough to let Him do heart surgery while healing your soul, mind, will, and emotions.

I have seen people who ask Jesus into their hearts, yet they are still going around the same cycles. Why that is, is that there is a wound in their soul. The Bible says in 3 John 1:2, "Dear friend, I pray that you may enjoy good health and that all may go well with you, even as your soul is getting along well."

First, let me note that the Apostle John was addressing us as friends. The Bible is not harsh, demanding, "Don't do this, don't do that." In all actuality, it is true freedom from the shackles of sin that separate us from a Holy, loving Father. The living Word of God is meant to be a love letter and a manual to live by.

There are many accounts in the Bible of people who loved God but made some bad choices, as you and I have. Look at King David, a man after God's heart. He had an affair with another man's wife and then had the husband killed! Now, what we do know about David is that he had a repentant heart. He was humble enough to realize that He could not live righteously without the Lord.

I want to point out that the people of Israel cried out for a King, and when Saul was made King, the people became the standard. Whereas the Lord picked David, and the Lord was the standard. Saul cared too much about what people were doing when they began to scatter in 1 Samuel 13.

1 Samuel 13:8-14 says, "He waited seven days, the time set by Samuel; but Samuel did not come to Gilgal, and Saul's men began to scatter. So he said, 'Bring me the burnt offering and the fellowship offerings.' And Saul offered up the burnt offering. Just as he finished making the offering, Samuel arrived, and Saul went out to greet him. 'What have you done?' asked Samuel. Saul replied, 'When I saw

that the men were scattering and that you did not come at the set time, and that the Philistines were assembling at Mikmash, I thought, Now the Philistines will come down against me at Gilgal, and I have not sought the Lord's favor. So, I felt compelled to offer the burnt offering' 'You have done a foolish thing,' Samuel said. 'You have not kept the command the Lord your God gave you; if you had, he would have established your Kingdom over Israel for all time. But now your Kingdom will not endure; the Lord has sought out a man after his own heart and appointed him ruler of his people because you have not kept the Lord's command.'"

Only the priest was to offer the burnt offering, but Saul disobeyed because of pressure, and Samuel not arriving when he thought he would. What you do during a delay will reveal what is truly in you. He took it upon himself to handle the precious things when he was not authorized. Saul cared too much about how things appeared rather than obeying the divine order from the Lord. David just wanted to ensure his heart was right before the Lord. Both men sinned, but one knew how desperate he was for the mercy of God.

When we fall short, do we run away, disregarding that we trespassed against the Lord? Or do we run towards Him, crying out for mercy? When we run away and ignore it as no big deal, it hardens the heart. Little by little, we stray further from being sensitive to His precious Holy Spirit. My friends, this is dangerous. Be quick to repent, knowing that in 1 John 1:9, the Bible says, "If we confess our sins, He is faithful and just and will forgive us our sins and purify us from all unrighteousness."

The Lord knows that if He did not send Jesus, His spotless lamb, to die for our sins, we would not be able to live according to His righteousness. Does that mean we are perfectly right when we accept Him and wear His robe of righteousness? Not exactly. We are justified or in right standing with God, purchased by Christ's blood. Sanctification is something that the Lord does with us. There is a seed within you that is being cultivated daily by prayer, the Word, worship (or, as I like to call it, WARSHIP), and spending time with the Father. This seed grows to where the world and sin no longer look enticing! 1 Peter 1:23 says, "For you have been born again, not of perishable seed, but of imperishable, through the living and enduring word of God."

The more you grow in intimacy, which I like to say, "into me, you see," the more you will not want to hurt the Father, the Son, or the Holy Spirit. This is sanctification, the action or process of being freed from sin or purified. Your spirit man's regeneration or new birth must be worked out in your soulish, fallen nature.

Salvation is a gift, but we must cooperate with sanctification if we are going to mature in faith.

2.
Lost

As I wrote earlier, I was saved as a kid but chose to go down a very dark road. While I was in middle school, like most kids, I tried to fit in and be the "cool kid." My mother loved me but tried to be my friend more than a disciplinarian. I remember wishing there had been more order in the home, even as a kid. Revelation 3:19 says, "Those whom I love, I rebuke and discipline." Discipline is necessary!

Cycles are hard to break if you do not know any better. My mother believed that if my friends came to our home and drank alcohol, she could protect us. She always said she would rather have us be in the house than on the streets. In middle school, I began to have a few friends over at a time, and we would drink and sometimes smoke marijuana.

During this time, my mother began having an affair with my friend's father. The son would come over and drink with me and my friends. Little did we know he happened to be going through a depression behind closed doors. I knew his grades were not going well, and he and his girlfriend had broken up. With everything that was going on, he committed suicide.

This tragedy was devastating for the community and the beginning of my spiraling into a dark depression. Word had gotten to his father that my mom was letting us drink at the house, and the police officers had been informed of it. Not long after my friend committed suicide, I had a few friends over, and we had been drinking. Later in the evening, my mother had taken some of the kids home, and when we got back to our house, it was being raided by the police.

After pulling up, my mom exited the car and was escorted to one of the police cars. My heart sank. I knew that my life as I knew it was going to be flipped upside down. The police officers searched the house and found some alcohol and two marijuana plants on my parents' back porch. One of the kids at our home had some marijuana on him, so the police officers initially thought that there was not only the distribution of alcohol to minors but also marijuana.

After interrogating everyone, the cops learned that the alcohol was what my mom had been providing. However, she did know there was marijuana being used in the house; she was not distributing it. After the police officers left that night, I took a whole bottle of aspirin in hopes that I would not wake back up. By the grace of God, I woke up the next day completely unharmed!

We lived in a lovely community, not because we had a lot of money, but because my mom liked to try to live on the "up and up." My parents often argued about money, and it always seemed like material things were something my mom tried to use to fill a void that only God could fill.

For days news reporters were coming by to try to get information. The newspaper labeled my mother the "Marijuana Mom," along with some false and true accusations. I felt like I was in a horrible nightmare! I encountered a lot of trauma as a kid, but this is when I completely went numb. The depth of my being was utterly shaken to the core.

I could no longer hang out with the good kids in the community and was completely ostracized. A few parents were still good to me, but I was judged entirely and even had a mother in the community tell me I killed my friend who committed suicide.

I became so angry with God. Before, I had been an honor roll student, was in dance class since I was four, had a modeling contract in Washington DC, and had all these hopes and aspirations. Still, after the publicity of what happened with my mom, I no longer wanted to go out in public. It was so publicized that it even reached CNN News. I felt like everything going well in my life was ruined, and I was judged as a kid for something that never should have happened.

My mother went to trial and received four counts of contributing to the delinquency of minors, plus charges for possession of marijuana. The judge ended up suspending a lot of the time, but she still had been sentenced to 5 years in prison. There was a point where child protective services wanted to take me from my dad as well, but they opted to allow me to stay with him since he did not know the whole of what my mom was allowing in the house.

From this point is when my rebellious years kicked into full throttle. I felt as if my reputation was already ruined and people already believed I was a drug addict, then why not live up to what people already believed? I began to drink even more heavily. When before, it was only occasionally on the weekend. I started smoking cigarettes, when before I could not stand even being in the same car when my parents smoked. Smoking cigarettes calmed my nerves, although what I actually needed was inner healing. I started sneaking out in the middle of the night, stealing my dad's vehicle so that I could go downtown to party. I had a lot of freedom to come and go because my dad worked a lot.

When my mom allowed us to drink at the house, at twelve years old, I lost my virginity. I remember how devastated I was the following day and cried to my mother. Although I was not living for God, I still had Jesus in my heart, and deep down, I wanted to live right. I had not slept with anyone for a while after that, but then I met a young man who I believed at the time to be the love of my life. I became co-dependent on this boy, and we had a serious relationship. I was only fifteen, and he was seventeen years old, but we practically lived like we were married. This relationship turned into abuse in many forms. There was physical abuse when he would break out into fits of rage. Then there was emotional abuse with lies and cheating. To think that I was so involved at such an early age is completely crazy to me now! I look at children at that age now and think, what was I doing? It blows my mind.

I grew up entirely too fast, but the beauty of my life now is that God has restored my innocence and given me back a childhood even in my thirties. He restores the years the enemy tried to steal (Joel 2:25). The years that you may have been in rebellion and feel that you wasted time, know that God is a redeemer, and He is the best at restoring you internally and externally.

This boy and I were together for a couple of years. Finally, I had enough of the abuse. Coming out of that relationship, I became promiscuous and did not think twice about it. From being molested as a child, I always felt like I could not say no and owed people a part of me. I felt like I was an object. I was looking for "love" or what I thought to be "love" in ALL the WRONG places!

Being around perversion growing up and seeing so much infidelity in the home caused me to have a skewed view of love that, in actuality, was lust. I did not know the true, pure love of Christ. If you have dealt with any form of sexual abuse or have seen a lot of perversion growing up, I want you to know it is not your fault that you were brought up in these environments and encountered these things; you were a child. It took me years to forgive myself and realize that I was innocent in the matter. Jesus took all guilt and shame at the cross; release it to Him!

When I was a kid, there was a close family that would allow me to spend the night over at their house, especially when my parents would get into altercations. Their home was a safe place until, one night, their son molested me when I was six years old. I kept it to myself for many years until I was with my parents at a restaurant at eighteen, and we ran into him. I remember getting into the car, and my face had this cold, almost distant look. I felt completely numb from the inside out. Then I burst into tears confessing to my parents what had happened to me as a child.

When a child, or even an adult, goes through sexual abuse, the enemy, the adversary of our soul, would rather us keep hush-hush and allow those inner wounds to fester. When keeping these deep, dark secrets to ourselves, we try to process them alone, which becomes a root cause of many other destructive behaviors. I like to say, "You may know the fruit that someone may be bearing, but you may not know the root or the reason a person is acting in a particular way."

For example, you may know a child acting out in anger, but you may not know that he has an alcoholic father that abuses him mentally and physically at home. Your environment growing up affects how you operate in the world. The good news is that with God's help and healing, we can rest assured that He desires that our innermost being be whole and that we experience total freedom from all trauma and past hurts! When we have a love encounter with the Creator of the universe, there is no doubt because we have had a divine intervention with a God, who is indeed love!

The Lord does not delight in us going through painful things and being mistreated. He is a just God and desires to heal us and make us whole through the blood of Jesus.

At an early age, pornography was left on our family computer. After it had been opened, ads would begin to pop up continually. This sparked curiosity. I became addicted to the adrenaline rush that pornography gave me. It opened a world of perversion, where I believe a spirit of lust had begun to attach to me. This feeling of being an object of affection and only being worth what I could give someone held me captive.

It is vital to guard what we look at and listen to because it opens doors to the enemy. Matthew 6:22-23 says, "The eye is the lamp of the body. If your eyes are healthy, your whole body will be full of light. But if your eyes are unhealthy, your whole body will be full of darkness. If the light within you is darkness, how great is that darkness!"

Increasingly, the culture is exploiting sexual perversion to the point where it is completely normalized, but this, my friend, is not normal. We live in an hour where people call good evil and evil good.

If you are a young lady or man exposed to sexual perversion and pornography at an early age, I want you to know that Jesus does not shame you. His hand is extended in mercy, desiring to wash you with His blood. The blood of Jesus will wash your consciousness, restore your innocence, and make you pure. I want to share a passage from the Bible about a woman who was caught in adultery.

John 8:1-11 says, "But Jesus went to the Mount of Olives. At dawn he appeared again in the temple courts, where all the people gathered around him, and he sat down to teach them. The teachers of the law and the Pharisees brought in a woman caught in adultery. They made her stand before the group and said to Jesus, 'Teacher, this woman was caught in the act of adultery. In the Law, Moses commanded us to stone such women. Now what do you say?' They were using this question as a trap in order to have a basis for accusing him. But Jesus bent down and started to write on the ground with his finger. They kept on questioning him, he straightened up and said to them, 'Let any one of you who is without sin be the first to throw a stone at her.' Again he stooped down and wrote on the ground. At this, those who heard began to go away one at a time, the older ones first, until only Jesus was left, with the woman still standing there. Jesus straightened up and asked her, 'Woman, where are they? Has no one condemned you?' 'No one, sir,' she said."

Jesus does not condemn you! The enemy tries to get us to sin, makes it look enticing, and then throws shame on us. Jesus came to free us from shame and does not treat us harshly. Our Savior died so we could approach the throne of grace boldly (Hebrews 4:16).

We can trust the goodness of the Lord in the land of the living! Adam and Eve, when they began to speak with the tempter, hid after they disobeyed God. They knew the goodness of God, but when they started to talk to the enemy, everything became distorted. The way we view the Lord is vital to our walk with Him. Do not believe the lies of the devil. God has amazing things in store for you as you walk out on this life journey with Him.

I think about how quickly I grew up and even how today's culture is rampant with sex, witchcraft, and all the enemy wants to fill us up with so that we will never know our true identity in the Lord. Satan knows that nothing will stop us when we grasp who we are in Christ! That is why it is vital to get into the Word of God and let it get deep within you so that you will be secure in who you are in Christ. Parents, guard your children's eyes and ears and yourself! Do not allow culture to shape your children; let the Word of God shape them.

Do not let what happened to you, what people did, or even what you did affect what God wants to do in your life. Repent of the things that you have done in the past, plead the blood of Jesus, and look forward. That may have been what you did, but that is not who you are at your core.

Jesus came so that heavy weights would not bind us. Matthew 11:28-30 says, "Come to me, all you who are weary and burdened, and I will give you rest. Take my yoke upon you and learn from me, for I am gentle and humble in heart, and you will find rest for your souls. For my yoke is easy, and my burden is light." Lay your cares and burdens at the cross.

One of our number one challenges, at least in my life, has been letting go of the past and genuinely accepting the Word of God. It says in Philippians 3:13-14, 13, "Brothers and sisters, I do not consider myself yet to have taken hold of it. But one thing I do: Forgetting what is behind and straining toward what is ahead, I press on toward the goal to win the prize for which God has called me heavenward in Christ Jesus." If the Lord forgot your past and has covered you with His blood, you can move forward into the destiny He has called you to.

Refrain from staying stuck rehearsing situations from the past but push forward with endurance and perseverance! Jesus has given us victory on the cross, but you must exercise that authority on the Earth, or the devil will use you as a punching bag. Please do not fall for his tricks and accusations. You are worthy of love, hope, and a future.

As a child, I remember hearing my mother speak about how she looked or about her body, and I began to take notice. Then, as children do, I began repeating what I saw—looking in the mirror to see if I looked thin or pretty enough. This was one of the seeds sown into my life that caused me to have a food issue, whether eating too much or too little. Also, with being in dance and modeling as a child, there was always a bit of pressure put on me to be thin. After my mother went to prison, I had gotten down to 114 pounds at 5'9". Food was something that I felt I could control, while everything else seemed to be spiraling out of control.

That was over two decades ago, and now with all the airbrushed social media and ads everywhere, there is much more pressure to look a certain way that is not even real. Your worth is never in what you look like but in your heart that your loving Savior transforms.

For years, I put so much emphasis on my looks, and it never satisfied me. Complete vanity. 1 Timothy

2:9 says, "Likewise, I want women to adorn themselves with proper clothing, modestly and discreetly, not with braided hair and gold or pearls or costly garments." I have heard the saying, "Modest is the hottest," and to the daughters of the Most High, you are royalty, and keeping yourself covered is beautiful. If you do not know that you are to be respected, you will lower your standards to what you have been told or what you have been through. But you have been chosen and accepted into the Kingdom. Your Beloved sees you fearfully and wonderfully made!

With all that I had seen as a child, I was confused about homosexuality. I will tell you right now in love that God has made it clear in His Word that homosexuality is indeed a sin and is an abomination. Don't you find it ironic that the theme for the month dedicated to LGBTQ is "pride?" Pride is the very sin that kicked Lucifer out of Heaven. The

Bible speaks on coming before the Lord humbly. For years, because of the confusion I had seen growing up, I believed the lie that I was bi-sexual.

When I was in jail, I asked the Lord, after reading the Scriptures, "Lord, if your Word is true about homosexuality, show me." And do you know what He said to my heart? "Humble yourself before me and lay it down." Many say, "I have been born this way," and "Cannot change."

In John 3:3-8, Jesus talks to the Jewish leader, Nicodemus, about being born again. "Jesus replied, 'Very truly I tell you, no one can see the Kingdom of God unless they are born again.' 'How can someone be born when they are old?' Nicodemus asked. 'Surely they cannot enter a second time into their mother's womb to be born!' Jesus answered, 'Very truly I tell you, no one can enter the Kingdom of God unless they are born of water and the Spirit. Flesh gives birth to flesh, but the Spirit gives birth to spirit. You should not be surprised at my saying, you must be born again. The wind blows wherever it pleases. You hear its sound, but you cannot tell where it comes from or where it is going. So, it is with everyone born of the Spirit."

We are all born one way, but we must be born again. You must let go of any lie you believe and ask the Lord to change your thoughts to His. This is what we call the renewing of the mind, as I mentioned earlier from Romans 12:2. The Creator of the universe did not make a mistake with you. Do you not believe if He created you a specific sex from birth, that was His intention? Confusion is not of God. If you need clarification in this area, ask the Lord for clarity.

When I humbled myself before God and gave Him the mindset that I was attracted to women, He set me free, forever taking those thoughts and feelings. God loves you and all sinners alike, but He hates sin! Do not be deceived in this area. True love has boundaries to protect your soul from the traps of the enemy. None of what I am sharing is to bring any guilt. My heart in authoring this book is to bring light and for people to know the Truth that will set them free.

As a friend of my parents babysat me, her kids had me watch a horror movie at an early age. This incident opened the door to fear and torment. I would have nightmares and run to my parents' room in the middle of the night, scared for my life. These experiences shaped my life at an early age, and not for the good. The enemy was infiltrating my thoughts and feelings, leading to wrong actions. These experiences were rooted in issues that continued for years until the Lord did a deep work in my soul. Fear wants to keep you in a box, but the Spirit of the Lord wants to liberate you! 2 Timothy 1:7 says, "For the

Spirit God gave us does not make us timid, but gives us power, love, and self-discipline."

For years after watching that first horror movie, I would love the thrill of watching them and then wonder why I had anxiety. It was not until my spiritual eyes were awakened to the light that I saw all the open doors to demons as a child. I even had an ouija board at an early age and was trying to conjure up the dead. Do not, I repeat, do not mess with tarot cards, psychics, ouija boards, and things alike! You are allowing the enemy access to your life through these practices. If you do not know, you do not know; there is grace for you now. Stop them and repent for it.

The Bible says in Hosea that we are destroyed for lack of knowledge. I genuinely loved God for years, but no one told me these hard truths. In our culture, witchcraft is thrown around as if it were no big deal. The Bible is clear that we are to seek the

Lord for our destinies. Jesus died on the cross so that we could have Godly counsel through the Holy Spirit within us. He is the way. We must choose life and walk in it. Even so, Jesus died for all sinners, the witch, the satanist, the heathen, and we should always have a heart of compassion and not judgment towards them. We have all fallen short of the grace of God, and we need to pray that those whom the cunningness of the enemy has deceived would be loosed from wickedness.

I opened many demonic doors in my early twenties seeking my future through tarot cards. I was seeking help from the outside, not realizing that the One who created me wanted to speak to me about the destiny He had for me. Around this time, I had gotten into a car accident that totaled my vehicle, my mother had been in jail, and my dad had lost his job. There seemed to be so much happening at once. We needed help, and I was desperate.

I had a tarot card reading that said I would meet a man soon that would help me financially. Not too long after that, I had been working at a Hooters on Valentine's Day. There was a man I had been serving at one of my tables who spoke about how he did not know it was Valentine's Day and asked if I would be his Valentine. He left a large tip, and the next day, I received a dozen roses with his number on the card, saying "Happy Valentine's Day," with his number.

In the natural, this looked appealing, but deep down, I knew it was all wrong. It reminds me of the saying, "All that glitters is not gold." Nonetheless, I ended up going on a date with him without having any peace in my heart. He bought me a beautiful necklace and began talking about buying me a car, all on the first date. I realized later in our relationship that the middle of the VIN number of the vehicle he ended up buying me was 666.

See, the enemy masquerades as an angel of light, and we must be discerning by the Spirit. I lived in blatant sin, but the Holy Ghost tried to warn me even then. We dated and soon became engaged. I had an $80,000, 5-carat ring on my finger, but I was empty inside. All looked good outside, but this was clearly not God's plan for my life. I had the money, car, trips, and anything material I wanted, but I still had a void that only the Lord could fill.

While with this man, I spun out of control on drugs like never before. I had been to drug rehab for thirty days in Williamsburg, Virginia, and I remember thinking about some of the people there, "How could they shoot up drugs with a needle? I would never do that." Not too long after that, I found myself shooting up heroin at a crazy amount a day. I remember waking up in a drug house after not speaking to my loved ones for days, thinking, "This is no way to live; I am dead inside but do not know how to get out." The enemy had put out bait, and I took the bait. I ended up in a far worse condition than I had ever been in.

It was not until I later went to jail after my fiancé and I had split up, that my spiritual eyes could see the doors I had opened to satan. The Lord spoke to my heart, "Jennifer if you are going to fulfill the call of God on your life, you must sever this relationship." Soul ties are real, and who (and what) we are connected to matters.

Fear and anxiety were something that I thought I had to live with until I encountered the power of God that set me free. Jesus wants you whole in your emotions and stable. There is wisdom and boundaries that are in place to protect your soul. God has given us free will to make choices. He is not a dictator but desires us to want to love Him and have a relationship with Him.

Daily, we ought to ask the Holy Spirit to help us to make wise choices to help us become more like Christ. If I do not believe Jesus would sit down and watch a bloody horror movie, representing death, when He is the very Truth and the Life, then I pray that you and I would not want to watch these things too. The more you fall in love with Jesus, the less appealing darkness looks. The more you are filled with light, the more you want no part with evil or even the appearance of evil.

It is not about being legalistic or that the Lord does not want you to have fun. It is about protecting you from allowing entry to the enemy in any area of your life. Jesus' blood defeated death, hell, and the grave, but if you give the enemy legal access through your choices, you must take responsibility and say enough is enough.

The Lord says, "Come higher, and leave the world behind." The more you leave the things of this world, the greater the life of God will implode within you. God is a good God, and when people say, "God has a good plan," it may seem like some cliché thing they say. In all honesty, He has an amazing destiny ahead for you if you cling to Him tightly, not being swayed by the temptations in this life.

When we invest in what lasts for eternity, our souls will be truly satisfied. This life and its "successes," whether a job, money, or self-promotion, will never fulfill you and will never be able to give you your identity. Only through Christ Jesus alone will you find who you were always created to be before the foundations of the Earth.

Prayer

Lord, I forgive _____ that has wronged me.

I release them to you.

I repent of any door that I have opened to the occult,

I repent of looking at pornography, fornication before marriage,

Or any other sexual perversion.

Thank you for your mercy that is washing over me now.

I want to be led by you, Holy Spirit.

I forgive myself,

And ask you to help me live for you.

Amen.

3.

The Crossroad

In 2013, at twenty-three years old, I went to jail for my second DUI. I had just split up from my fiancé then and went off the deep end with alcohol, pills, and whatever I could get my hands on.

I had recently overdosed on heroin while shooting up in my car. Thank the Lord, the lady that had been with me took me to the hospital. She and the drug dealer could have left me for dead. I remember waking up with IVs hooked to me, not knowing what had happened. I do not remember a whole lot about being discharged. I just got up and left.

Not long after this, my fiancé took me to get an opiate blocker inserted under my skin at a local clinic.

Having this inserted would prevent me from feeling any effects from an opiate if I used them. First, though, I would have to detox from the Xanax and heroin I had been on. Boy, I was a force to be reckoned with during this time.

The truth is, I see it so clearly now, just how broken and empty I was when I was using. I wanted to fill the void and the hurt of my childhood. I tried to escape. I no longer wanted to deal with life as it was.

After my fiancé and I split up, I stayed at a hotel with a girlfriend of mine, living recklessly, until one day, everything changed. We had stopped at a stop light, and two white cars were lined up beside each other. One license plate said, "Who's God?" and the second said, "He is coming." The girl I was with looked at me and said, "That is for you." I remember looking perplexed like, "What in the world? What are the odds?"

Only He knows whether those license plates actually said that or whether the Lord changed them supernaturally to show me what He wanted to say to me. Either way, we both saw it, and it hit me like a ton of bricks. For weeks, the Lord would send people to warn me, even in my rebellion. "Jenn, you need to slow down," "Jenn, you need not to go there, etc." But I was stubborn and did not want to hear it.

Little did I know that at that time, my mother had been incarcerated, and some Pentecostal women were visiting the jail to do Bible study. They had been praying for me and asking God to intervene in my life, and my God did He! Later that evening, I was drinking hard liquor very heavily at a local bar. I ended up leaving the bar and began accelerating my vehicle to a whopping eighty-five mile-an-hour speed on a forty-five mile-an-hour road! Where I was going at that rate, I do not know. Lord knows I was not in my right mind! There was a police chase of five police cars behind me. I finally pulled over right in front of the hotel I had been staying at, where the police officers jumped out and pinned me to the ground.

I was well over the legal limit of alcohol and went to jail that night. I felt like my world was crashing in, but little did I know, this was my turning point. This was my crossroads and surrender, where the Lord met me in my mess and pursued me with His great love. Some may say they "found God," but He finds us. And He delights in helping us in times of need. Romans 5:8 says, "But God demonstrates his own love for us in this: While we were still sinners, Christ died for us."

After the court trial, I was sent to the local jail, where my mother was incarcerated. It turns out we ended up in the same jail cell, and anyone that has been locked up knows that does not happen. You are not supposed to be housed with family because it could possibly be a liability.

The Lord put me face-to-face with her while sober so that there could be some healing in our relationship. The Bible speaks about how He cannot forgive us when we do not forgive. Mercy is extended when we extend mercy (Matthew 6:15). When we are in unforgiveness, we allow bitterness, like a poison, to fester and infiltrate through our whole being. Keep yourself free of offense, with no contamination. Keep yourself fit to be a conduit of the life of God with no hindrance—a place where He can make His dwelling.

The Lord began to give me a fresh perspective of my mother being a child of God and all the turmoil she encountered growing up. Do not let your own unforgiveness keep you captive. Sometimes people see how someone may act or the fruit in their life, but they do not realize how they got to that place. Hurt people hurt people, and without healing in their souls, it is an entryway for the enemy to set up camp. Seeing my mother sober and happy in those months was refreshing. We laughed, and we cried. It was truly a divine setup, and I thank God for it.

While incarcerated, I was given a book by Katie Souza called "Key to Your Expected End." I realized that if God delivered and restored her from a life of hard knocks and drugs, He could do it for me. There had been a long time since the enemy had me thinking the lie that I could never be like those "church people." I would think, "I've done too much; I could never be pure." The Truth is we all fall short of the Glory of God, and not one is righteous. We receive Jesus' imputed righteousness when Christ comes into our hearts. Our righteousness is as filthy rags! So, trying to be "good" without the Holy Spirit that dwells inside us is like running in circles to no avail. It gets you nowhere!

I look back now and think, "My God, how did I live without the Power of God?" Now I cannot get enough of His Presence! Do not believe the lies that you could never be worthy of love. Jesus paid the price for ALL sin and no sin is more significant than another. When the accuser comes and tries to tell you what you are not, use your mouth and tell him he is right; we do not do everything right, but Jesus did, and we are in HIM!

Speak to the enemy, and do not let him push you around. For years I would allow him to bully my mind and emotions, and I would think the Word of God in my mind, but we must speak the Word aloud, the sword of the Spirit. As you do that, you will feel the atmosphere shift and begin to feel lighter. Proverbs 18:21 says, "The tongue has the power of life and death."

The devil wants to keep you weighed down with junk that is not yours to take on. Jesus paid the price so that we could be free and free indeed! We must catch the thought quickly to demolish the lie with the Truth before it becomes a stronghold. A stronghold is a place where a particular belief or ideology is firmly believed. That is why it is vital to know what the Word of God says so that we do not believe lies, allowing these seeds of thoughts to become fortified fortresses in our thinking.

For the three and a half months that I was locked up, I felt the most peace and joy that I had ever had in my entire life. To be so full of His Presence but yet, in adverse circumstances was a supernatural way that I had never known. I was more free in jail than I ever was in the streets! When I truly could forgive my mother and began to forgive myself, which was a big one, the weight lifted off my shoulders.

I felt lighter and knew God was Immanuel, "God with us." He had been with me all along and longed for me to turn, repent of my rebellion, and run into His loving arms. I could not comprehend how a God, even in my mess ups, still reached out His merciful hand after I had gone my own way so many times.

I am reminded of the prodigal son in Luke 15:21-24, "The son said to him, 'Father, I have sinned against Heaven and against you. I am no longer worthy to be called your son.' But the father said to his servants, 'Quick! Bring the best robe and put it on him. Put a ring on his finger and sandals on his feet. Bring the fattened calf and kill it. Let's have a feast and celebrate. For this son of mine was dead and is alive again; he was lost and is found.' So, they began to celebrate."

The Lord says in His Word that He throws our sins as far as the East is from the West. Psalm 103:11-12, "For as far as the heavens are above the earth, so great is His love for those who fear Him; as far as the east is from the west, so far has He removed our transgressions from us." East and West can never meet; what a beautiful picture of God's forgiveness! He completely separates us from our sins when He forgives us, never to come back to condemn us.

A lot of the time, we are the ones rehearsing the failures over and over, leaving us feeling stuck and in condemnation. That is not the God we serve! He is a just and Holy God, but when you repent and turn away from your sin, He is not holding you responsible. Jesus took the guilt and the condemnation of sin, which was nailed to the Cross on Calvary! Romans 8:1 says, "Therefore, there is now no condemnation for those who are in Christ Jesus." His shed Blood was and is the ultimate sacrifice. We must intentionally get our soulish, fleshly nature in line with what our Spirit man already knows is true.

The Word became so alive to me while in jail, and it amazed me how I could feel spiritually nourished after ingesting it day by day. It was my safe place, my daily bread. I began to think differently, and my heart overflowed with love and gratitude. What a new way of life! I knew about God, but His manifest Presence was so real, so tangible, that no one could tell me He was not good or real.

I would read Scripture for years, but it was different this time. I could feel the power and the light changing me from the inside out. It was no longer a "Religious duty." Reading the Word was something I delighted in and was hungry for daily. The Logos (written Word) and the Rhema (spoken Word) together changed my life. We need the person of the Holy Spirit to understand the Scriptures. Ask, and He will help!

When I was released from jail, I went to hang out with a guy that I had seen before jail. Knowing my spirit man did not want me to keep that relationship, I lacked peace. 1 Corinthians 15:33

speaks on how bad company corrupts good character, and we must be intentional about whom we surround ourselves with if we want to grow. It may be uncomfortable to fellowship with people who have had nothing in common with you previously and are on another level spiritually, but this is how we grow. If we do what we have always done, we will get what we always had.

Anyhow, I returned to this man, and we ended up drinking. By the night's end, I was left crying and bruised all over after an altercation. It was then that I realized that while I had gotten close to the Lord in jail, the enemy now had a target on me to take me back to where I was. He wanted to destroy the seeds that were sown in my heart.

I turned to the book of Jonah that night in tears, and the Lord reassured me He was giving me another chance to break with the old self. A few days later, I packed my stuff up and headed to stay with my dad in the country. I had no license but knew that it was the retreat I needed to get away from the world and get the world out of me. The Israelites were delivered from Egypt in a day, but it took forty years to get Egypt out of them.

My mother got out of jail shortly after I was released. She had been sober for a few days, then the doctor she had seen for years prescribed her a lethal dose of a painkiller called fentanyl. It baffled me that he would give her such a high dosage right after she got out. She did have a stroke in 2001 and was prescribed it for pain in her left leg, but she was an addict, and this medication left her like a walking zombie. I would be so upset that my mother was there physically, but she was not fully present when she was on this medication.

A day after she had taken the fentanyl after getting home from jail, I awakened with a horrible feeling. I remember running to the kitchen and seeing my mother's coffee on the kitchen counter. I then ran upstairs to find my mother barely breathing, with her lips purple and blue. By the time the medics had gotten there, she had passed away. I genuinely do not believe my mother wanted to die; she just thought she could handle the amount of painkiller she had been on before her incarceration.

There was a lady police officer that had arrived on the scene that I had known from previous times when she had been called to our house. She immediately said, "This is going to be you!" I began to tell her that Jesus had changed my life, and I was no longer using drugs. Later the police officer came to me and apologized. The bottom line was that she was concerned I was continuing down that path.

Years prior, this very same police officer had been called to our house because my mother had drowned in our pool after we had been drinking. She hit her head on the incline after drinking alcohol mixed with Xanax and was knocked unconscious. My friend and I pulled her out, and I began to give her CPR. My mother was in a coma for a week after that and even saw a bright light in Heaven. My pop (Great Grandfather) looked down and told her she was not ready yet.

There had been another time this lady police officer was called, and I was fighting with my mother. While being up for days on multiple drugs, I freaked out and hit the police officer. I was entirely out of my right mind. She later reduced the charges, so I did not receive a felony. Needless to say, the police officer was concerned about my well-being. She wanted to make sure I was not still going down that dark path. I made it up in my mind that after my mom died from an overdose, the devil would pay! I was going to change the course of my family by the blood of Jesus!

The first two years after I first got out of jail were formative years. I read my Bible and sat with

Jesus for hours. The foundation of a building, as well as a foundation of anything for that matter, is of the utmost importance. The stronger the foundation in the Word and fellowship with the Person of Jesus through the Holy Spirit, the stronger your walk will be, with fruit that remains.

Not long after I got out of jail, one of the ladies visiting us in the jail when doing Bible study decided she would take me under her wing and disciple me. It is amazing to win a person to Jesus, but if people who are babes in Christ do not have the accountability, love, and help to walk in this journey with Christ, it gives room for the enemy to pull them back into bondage. We need the Body of Christ to assist us in this walk. It is not a once saved, "I got this, me and Jesus." We are not called to be an island on our own.

For me, I had such an independent way of doing things. I needed to humble myself to ask for help and realize that God wants us to have a community to grow with. Even as a kid, I felt I needed to grow up so quickly and take care of myself because I was put in adult situations and saw so much early on. I had this "fend for myself" mentality. Once we repent of our sins and receive Jesus into our hearts, our way of doing things must change.

You are no longer in the driver's seat of your life when you choose to surrender. It is a surrendering of old ways of thinking, old ways of doing things, and an all-out NEWNESS of life. The more we humble ourselves and yield to Him, the more the life of God can manifest in our lives. We can truly have as much of the Lord as we want. I like to say, "If you will give it all, you can have it all."

Jesus paid the price on the cross so that we could have all that we need in this life pertaining to life and godliness (2nd Peter 1:3). It is not as complicated as some perceive it to be. The simple Truth is to believe! Get the Word of God in you and ask for the Spirit of the Lord to change you into His image.

When you accept Christ, the seed of Truth is already in you, but your sanctification is being worked out daily as you yield. We come to Christ as we are but are never meant to stay as we are. It is a progressive journey where we go from Glory to Glory. The Lord Himself is glorious intrinsically, but also, He extrinsically offers us Glory as we spend time with Him and are molded more into His image.

One moment in the Glory, the manifest Presence of God, can change your whole life, more than striving to work hard all of your life. The Lord is good and wants you to enjoy His Presence! In Exodus, Moses said to the Lord he would not go into the Promise Land if he did not have the Lord's Presence. He knew that He had all He needed if He had the Lord. His Presence triumphed over the promises. All the other things are added when we put the Lord in His rightful place (Matthew 6:33).

Karen, the woman who took me under her wing, was persistent in getting me to church but never pushy. She genuinely cared about my soul and would go out of the way to get me to the house of God. So many times, she would know by the Spirit that I was going through something, and she would send me a text of encouragement.

The Lord sometimes may pop someone into your spirit, and it is meant for you to intercede. I learned this not long after I got out of jail. I was cleaning one day and began thinking of the movie *Mrs. Doubtfire*. I watched it as a kid, with the lead actor Robin Williams. It turns out that a day later, Robin died of suicide. The Lord was prompting me to pray for him, and he was teaching me to pray into what was in my spirit, which was *Mrs. Doubtfire,* but it was so much more than that. Lord, help us be so sensitive to your Spirit that when you show us a person or something, we pray into it.

The Bible says that when we do not know what to pray, we pray in the Spirit (Romans 8:26). At the time, my prayer language had not yet been in action, but it certainly would be birthed right around the corner. Refrain from getting into religious thinking that you must pray to the Lord in some form or fashion. Through Jesus, we can come to our Father boldly and talk to Him as a friend. Of course, this is a friend who is absolutely holy and divine, so we come in reverence, but He wants you to be real with Him and be vulnerable.

Our Father did not create man because He needed man; He created man because He wanted a relationship with man. You are wanted, and you are indeed valuable to Him! We can communicate openly with Him at all times of the day, and as we let down our guard, He can get into all the crevices that need

His outpouring of love and healing. Your whole soul, comprised of your mind, will, and emotions, matters to God! The Lord delights in every detail of the godly (Psalm 37:23).

4.

Glorious

What I share now is a night that truly marked me! Everything changed from this point on. I was invited to a revival at New Life Church in Farmville, Virginia. I remember there was resistance when trying to get there, which is even more of an indication you need to go get your blessing! I stood in worship as I heard other believers praying in the Spirit. I had never encountered "Praying in the Spirit." I thought to myself, "This is kind of different!"

The revivalist began to preach on Moses and the Glory of God. I asked in my heart for the Lord to show me His Glory, and He sure did! At the end of the service, there was an altar call, and the revivalist laid hands on me. I fell out on the ground, slain in the Spirit, which had never happened to me before. I wept for a good hour while other ministers prayed in the Spirit over me. The Lord was cleansing my soul with His precious touch.

When I got up from this encounter, everything looked brighter, as if I were walking on a cloud! I felt this exuberant joy and peace. I felt like it was Heaven on Earth. I truly encountered Glory, the manifest Presence of the Lord. The Kingdom of God, peace, joy, and righteousness in the Holy Ghost is already in you as a born-again believer (Romans 14:17). You need to draw from the flow within you, as Nancy Dufresne, a minister I like to glean from, says! We are not trying to get to something when we read the Bible; we read the Bible to reveal what we already have as believers. We fight from victory, never for victory. Jesus has won the battle; it is finished!

After I came out of the church from that revival, my dad picked me up, and I remember him looking at me concerned, asking, "Do I need to take you to Tuckers?" Mind you, Tuckers is not some resort! It is a mental institution that I had previously been to before I surrendered to Christ. I had been admitted there from hearing voices, and now I know demons were tormenting me because of all the doors I had opened through sin.

When you rebel against God's ways, you are no longer under the umbrella of protection. You do not get to do it your way and expect the Spirit to back you. The Bible shows us boundaries and is a love letter to protect, reprove and help us walk this out on the Earth. When my dad saw that I had been crying, he assumed something was wrong, when in all actuality, I had just had my first encounter with God's power and Glory! It completely rocked me, and from that point on, I was addicted to the Presence of God.

To be with my Beloved was my most treasured time. While in that season at my dad's house, my dad would even ask me, "Aren't you going to watch television anymore?" I would stay in my room often while reading the Word and being still before Him. One of my favorite Scriptures is Psalm 46:10, "Be still and know that He is God." We live in a fast-paced society with many distractions begging for our attention, when the Lord wants to woo us into His chamber and speak to His beloved.

Stillness and silence are spiritual disciplines that are vital and what the Western Church needs more of. How do we know the steps that He would have us take if we are not still before Him to hear the next command of action? It is good to be excited and full of zeal, but at the same time, excitement does not equal the will of God for your life. You need to take time to hear His assignments specifically for your life.

After that encounter, I began to seek this King of Glory. I decided not long after this encounter that I would get water baptized. I had been baptized as a child, but honestly, I did not know what I was doing or what it meant. Water baptism symbolizes that you are willing to follow Jesus and have your life match His will for you. After getting water baptized this time, I came out of the water and immediately felt lighter. My sin and my old life were left in that baptismal tank.

Again, I felt like I was walking on a cloud, and His Presence was so heavy. All day after the water baptism, I was in complete awe and wonder of the Lord. After years of shame and guilt being lifted off me, I felt so pure and innocent, which only the blood of Jesus can do!

5.

Smash the Rearview

Oh, how the blood of Jesus makes us pure. I am thankful that shame and condemnation can no longer keep me silent. I believe it took me so long to get the ball rolling on this book (the Lord had spoken to me about it for about five years) because I was still dealing with some shame concerning parts of my past. I realize that the purpose of authoring this book is to bring hidden things to light, break the enemy's power over lives, and bring much healing in my life by writing things down that have happened.

The beauty of it is that although these things happened, I am no longer bound and no longer stuck.

This is my deep desire for you as well. When the Bible says, ALL things new, the Lord means it! I do not know why sometimes that may seem more of a reality for others, but my friend, it is for YOU too! He has not forgotten about you, and He is for you.

For years even after being saved, I still had trouble believing God had erased all my past as if it had never happened. The truth is, I had forgiven others, but I do not think deep down I had forgiven myself. The same grace we give to others, we must extend that to ourselves. Our Father loves us so much, and His Word says we are made in His image. When we think wrong thoughts and harbor self-hatred towards ourselves, we call Him a liar! Whoa, right?! Trust me, I get it. I have gone through much healing, and has it happened all at once? For me, it has not, but it can happen quickly when we begin to align our thoughts with His thoughts toward us.

Recently I was in a small group when the Lord showed me something that needed healing in my soul. I listened to worship music for the rest of the night as my Abba ministered to me as I wept. The following day, I looked over at our kitchen counter, and one onion was sitting there alone. I remember immediately how for years people would tell me that healing is like that of an onion with many layers.

Do not be discouraged with yourself. Remember that we are all on the potter's wheel, and sometimes, some more forming occurs as the rough edges are smoothed. However, know that He is making you into a beautiful masterpiece, and you have not seen your best days yet!

I recall one time I was sitting in our living room when one of my friends messaged me to pray for her Aunt Pam because she had a hammer fall on her while she was on a ladder. Of course, I began to pray, but when I would say "hammer," I laughed and laughed hysterically. I thought, "Lord, I am trying to pray and be serious, but this is not working. Whenever I say 'hammer,' I laugh non-stop!" The Lord will have me laughing at some of the most serious of times just to make religion mad!

Joy is our strength, and the Bible says in Psalm 2:4, "The One enthroned in heaven laughs; the Lord scoffs at them." Our Father in Heaven is laughing at our enemies. When things may not work out as planned, you know what I say, laugh! I like what Mark Hankins says, "Joy is the serious business of heaven." Even in times of suffering, there is encouragement in Christ. That is how we can be as well when things go sideways.

Consider how Paul and Silas were in jail in Acts 16:23-26: "After they had been severely flogged, they were thrown into prison, and the jailer was commanded to guard them carefully. When he received these orders, he put them in the inner cell and fastened their feet in the stocks. About midnight, Paul and Silas were praying and singing hymns to God, and the other prisoners were listening to them. Suddenly, there was such a violent earthquake that the foundations of the prison were shaken. At once, all the prison doors flew open, and everyone's chains came loose."

We can be in the most adverse situations and still be in joy! They remained in a state of praise to the Lord, knowing He was bigger than the situation at hand. This is the supernatural way of a believer. Look to the Lord and know that no matter what you are going through, you are hidden with Him in Christ Jesus.

The following day after my friend asked me to pray for her aunt, I began reading a devotional by Heidi Baker called *Joyful Surrender*. She starts talking about knowing your identity and realizing whatever you did in the past is now erased. Then in the following sentence, she says, "You think the sledgehammer of Heaven is falling on you. But do you know where it is hitting? Your rearview mirror!" Then, yet again, I busted out laughing. The Lord showed me why I laughed so much when I prayed about the hammer falling.

Not only was He showing me that Pam would be okay and that He had it taken care of, but He was also showing me, "Hey girl, let it go!!" Isn't it amazing how the Lord can speak in many different ways when our spiritual senses are attuned to His Spirit? That is what a relationship is about. The Lord does not want our attention only in church! That is Religion. He wants to get all in your business and speak to you daily. Isn't that beautiful? This is the intimacy that He has called us to.

In my late teens, my mom had just gotten out of prison. We had to go through a lot of adjustments during this time. She went to prison when I was twelve and returned home when I was eighteen. When returning home, she wanted to treat me like I was still a kid, which did not go over well. I lived as if I were an adult and had done my own thing since she had been gone.

We decided we were going to try to do some counseling at a church for some healing in our relationship. The lady that did our counseling had known us for a while and asked me if she and her husband paid for me to do a young adults youth camp, would I go. I decided that I would and that anything would be better than the chaos and torment I was going through.

When I went to this camp, I experienced some deliverance, but my soul was still not whole. I remember thinking I could not be good like "those good church people." The enemy had me believing such lies that I could never live a holy life. I left the camp changed, though, desiring not to smoke weed anymore, smoke cigarettes, and truthfully, I did not want to have sex anymore.

After finding some freedom, I wanted to attempt to do things another way but did not believe my boyfriend at the time would understand. My friends, things can be different! Do not fall into the trap of thinking it cannot, in trying to please people, just to go along to get along. You have a right to take the reins of your life through Christ Jesus.

I am sharing these stories because I want you not to go down the road I went down, and if you have gone down these paths, know that there is a way out. Matthew 12:43:45 says, "When an impure spirit comes out of a person, it goes through arid places seeking rest and does not find it. Then it says, 'I will return to the house I left.' When it arrives, it finds the house unoccupied, swept clean, and put in order. Then it goes and takes with it seven other spirits more wicked than itself, and they go in and live there. And the final condition of that person is worse than the first. That is how it will be with this wicked generation."

These verses above became very real to me after coming home from this camp. I went back to living with my boyfriend, and even though my spirit man wanted to do right, I was pulled back by my flesh and even more tormented than before. The enemy had a target out on my back as he saw I attempted to get free. Though it was amazing to have some relief while at the camp, I wish someone would have helped me more in the after stages of the deliverance because I went right back, and it was much worse.

At this time, voices, which I know now to be demons, were conversing with me to go down to the strip club and prostitute my body. I had an old friend who was a dancer, and I knew she had a friend who owned a strip club. He was known in the city as a notorious bad boy. For days, these conversations would play in my mind to go into the city and use my body for money. It was as if a magnetic pull of evil was trying to get me to do it. I eventually caved in. The wild thing is, deep down, I never enjoyed it. I was dead inside and knew what I was doing was wrong, but the pull was intense because I had given the enemy legal access through my sin.

The enemy wants to kill, steal, and destroy your life (John 10:10). Get free and make the hard choices to STAY free or suffer the consequences of being tormented even more. The reality is that this happens worldwide, and people may not want to talk about it. Money is the root of all evil when it becomes the central focus. The bottom line, you cannot serve both God and money.

God indeed has a good plan for your life, and He conquered death, hell, and the grave. That does not negate the fact that we still must contend for the promises; we still must take ground for the Kingdom.

The Bible says in Matthew 11:12, "From the days of John the Baptist until now, the kingdom of heaven has been subjected to violence, and violent people have been raiding it." We must be aggressive and not expect being a passive Christian to go well with us. We can be Christian and live weakly and depleted because we lack knowing what is already ours! May we be those who do not settle. Through Jesus' blood, we have all that we need. We must believe that it is already ours.

Smash the rearview and step forward into destiny!

Prayer

Lord, I thank You that You make all things new,

Wash me with your blood.

I am a new creation in you,

And my past has no hold on me.

I declare that I am free to move forward into my destiny,

In the peace and the joy that you have provided for me.

In Jesus' name,

Amen.

6.

Accepted

When you surrender your life to Jesus, you are a child of God. I do not know if you had your mother around as a child or if your father was in your life, but what I do know is that our Father in Heaven accepts you in the beloved. What does the word "Beloved." mean? It means "dearly loved." Ephesians 1:5-6 says, "He predestined us for adoption to sonship through Jesus Christ, in accordance with His pleasure and will— to the praise of His glorious grace, which He has freely given us in the One He loves."

Before the foundation of the world, our Father God had you on His mind. Before Adam and Eve disobeyed and lost dominion in the garden, the Father had a redeeming plan of love for us to be restored to Him. The enemy's voice wants to put a heavy weight on you and accuse you of what you did and who you are not. That is why knowing your identity in Jesus is essential so you will not fall for the enemy's schemes.

You may feel lonely, but the Truth is, you are never alone. You may feel sad, but the Truth is, He is the lifter of your head. There have been seasons of my life where the Lord will show Himself in new ways. There are many facets to who He is; He reveals Himself how He chooses. I have seen the Lord as a faithful Father who truly provides all that we need spiritually, emotionally, mentally, or physically.

When I was eighteen, I had just graduated high school and got pregnant. My parents kept persuading me to have an abortion. My boyfriend was dealing drugs, and I was not stable. The thought of killing a child within me broke my heart, though. I had done so many drugs and been in complete rebellion against God, but the idea of murdering my child was devastating.

I went to the abortion clinic a couple of times after my parents insisted that if I did not have this abortion, my life would be ruined. They threatened to take my car away and told me I would need to find another place to live. I finally caved into the pressure, which was entirely against my will. After the abortion, my boyfriend, my mother, and I went to his trailer, where my mother began to drink. With tears flowing down my face, I decided to go for a walk to clear my head. When I got back to the trailer, I knew something was not right in my heart.

My boyfriend looked at me and said, "Your mom is wrong." Even in my rebellion, I knew what had happened. I knew by the Spirit that she had uncovered that the man I thought to be my Dad for eighteen years was not my biological father. I blurted it out in the bedroom to my boyfriend, and he was shocked that I knew what had happened.

My mom mentioned to him that he might not be the father of my child because we broke up for some time and that Ray, the man who raised me, was not my father. I then confronted my mother and my family. None of them would tell me he was not my biological father. I just wanted the truth. I knew my father, Ray, raised me, but I wanted to know where I came from.

I became so angry and bitter that none of my family members would be upfront with me. It was not until weeks later, while my mother had been drinking that I had asked her about my biological father. She said they had moved to Orlando and found out she was three months pregnant. When she told him about the pregnancy, he said he did not want any more children. (He had two older sons that were grown.) Then he told her to have an abortion.

My mom, at eighteen, decided she would keep me and moved to Georgia to live with my Great Aunt Carol while she was pregnant. She knew if she moved back to Virginia, where I am from, other bad influences would not be good for her to be around.

My mother moved to Virginia right before I was born, where she met my father, Ray, who raised me. He has always been in my life, and I am so thankful I had a father figure growing up. We have been so close through the years, and he has added so much value to my life. Deep down, though, I was angry that I was lied to, regardless of why it was hidden. The way I found out, in a time of deep despair, after aborting the child within my womb was almost too much to bear.

Time went by, and I found my biological father on Facebook. I reached out to him, not wanting anything from him, but honestly just wanting to know my family heritage. He never responded, but I believe that the Lord, in His goodness, will shield us from people and situations that we may think will be good but ultimately will cause detriment.

What is so beautiful is that the Lord has positioned me in Orlando, Florida, establishing me as I walk into my destiny. The very place where I was rejected in the womb is where the Lord redeemed my story. God has a way of bringing people into our lives that provide love and care in ways He knows we need. What we may lack in our biological family, He will provide in others. As you trust the Lord, He will bring those who are for you and will help love you to life.

Remember that the one who loves you the most, the lover of your soul, wants to be your everything. He could not love you any more than He loves you because our Father is love. If you have dealt with rejection from people that were supposed to be there for you, know that the heart of the Father is acceptance. You are always welcomed into His loving arms.

We must remember that we are flesh, and the reality is that we do not have it all together. Only He is good. When you know the Father's love and accept His love, it will flow through you to others. If you are wounded and operate out of a hurt soul, there is an entryway for wrong thinking, which, in turn, will cause wrong actions.

Having our souls healed by the healing oil of the Lord is so important that we can operate out of a place of wholeness. People can genuinely love you, but because of their brokenness, it is an access point for the demonic. Ephesians 6:12 says, "For our struggle is not against flesh and blood, but against the rulers, against the authorities, against the powers of this dark world and against the spiritual forces of evil in the heavenly realms." We cannot try to fight what is spiritual in natural ways. 2

Corinthians 10:4 says, "The weapons we fight with are not the weapons of the world. On the contrary, they have divine power to demolish strongholds." We must use the sword of the Spirit as our offensive weapon to demolish lies.

One day as I was at my Mama Laura's place in Alabama, we were worshipping, and the Holy Spirit had highlighted a piece of decoration that was in the front corridor that said, "Believe." He showed me the middle of the word "believe" had the word "lie" in it. Then He shared how our belief system in who He is and His character, will swallow up the lies that we have believed.

When we know our God and allow Him to reveal His nature to us, we can trust that He is indeed good! Religion says, "Do this, and God will accept you." Sonship says, "Jesus paid it all, just receive that you're accepted in the beloved." Religion will always enslave you. Sonship will always liberate you. Being a perfectionist is rooted in performance. Being faithful is rooted in obedience.

Prayer of Acceptance

Father, I thank you that I am your child.

I am no longer an orphan.

I am no longer rejected.

Today, I am accepted in the Kingdom of God,

I am fearfully and wonderfully made.

You receive me just as I am,

And you are making beauty out of ashes.

I choose to forgive those who have hurt me,

And I release them to you.

I ask you to make all things new in me.

In Jesus' name,

Amen.

7.

Trusting the Father

Learning to trust the Lord takes time, especially if people have hurt you and have allowed walls to form. Lately, the Lord has been speaking to me about His goodness. He does not just do good things; He is altogether GOOD. When Adam and Eve sinned, that is where the distorted views of God came into place. Adam and Eve were in the Garden of Eden, walking hand in hand with their maker and Father, but once they disobeyed, they immediately ran to hide. They hid because of the guilt and shame, but also, they began to see God in a wrong way. The Father called out to them by their names. He knew what they had done, and still, He pursued them.

They spoke with the tempter, sinned, and then hid. The enemy will try to tempt you; he will try to make it look enticing, and then once you have sinned, he will throw guilt and shame upon you. Thanks be to God, that by the shed blood of Jesus, we can now approach the throne of grace boldly. When we mess up, we can run to our Father's embrace and not away from Him. The blood of Jesus restored what Adam and Eve lost in the Garden, fellowship with our Father.

Do not allow your falling short to keep you from approaching the Lord. The Lord is always looking to restore His children. He desires to bless you in every area of your life, but if you do not believe that, you will have what you believe. That is why we are to have our minds renewed in the Word. If we do not get the Word in us, dividing the soul (mind, will and emotions) and the spirit, it will be hard to discern the leading of the Holy Spirit.

Jesus on the cross, said "It is finished," meaning ALL that we need in this life is wrapped up in HIM. When we receive Christ, we have a delightful inheritance. We need to be able to walk this out on the Earth as ambassadors of Heaven. Thank God this world is not our home, that as children of God we are passing through this life as pilgrims onto our heavenly reward.

We do not have to live lives of defeat as children of God. We can live lives of victory! We need revelation on how to walk it out. The Holy Spirit is sent to live in us to be our helper, so we can walk in all that the Father has for us. We must remember that the Holy Spirit is a person and can be trusted because He, Jesus, and the Father are one.

Many people want to know, "What is the will of God for me?" Don't we all want to see His destiny for us? His Word is His will, and you must know that as you allow the Word to wash you and change you, you will become more sharpened in your spirit man. Then when the Spirit of God is unctioning you, your spirit will bear witness.

Refrain from overcomplicating things in what, how, and when. When you allow the Word of God to change you and peace to be the umpire of your heart, the Spirit of God will lead you to where you need to be at the right time. I can testify of how the unfolding of the plan of God has taken place in my life as my spirit man has led me.

When you allow the Holy Spirit to lead you, do not allow your reasoning to override what the Lord has already spoken! It does not have to make sense in the natural, and most likely will not, but always be led by your spirit man as it bears witness to the Holy Spirit's promptings. Proverbs 3:5-6 says, "Trust in the Lord with all of your heart and lean not on your own understanding; in all your ways submit to him, and he will make your paths straight."

In 2018, I was serving the Lord faithfully at my local church in Powhatan, Virginia. I absolutely adored this church! Pastors Johnathan and Kristi Whichard are truly authentic. Years before the Lord moved me to their church, I had visited and loved the atmosphere. God was moving in that place! I had no idea that He would have me planted in their congregation years later.

Under their covering, I never once backslid in addiction. I had never even tasted alcohol since I had joined their congregation. It matters what you are connected to! Always be led by the Spirit when you are looking for a church. Do not look at how big or popular the church is. You want to ensure your leaders are men and women of integrity and preaching the uncompromising Word of God. It all flows from the head! And ministers, whatever you share with others, make sure you are also living up to that standard. Mama Laura says, "Eat what you serve." The walk of Holiness is a journey, but we should always look to grow in this area as we walk with Jesus.

During the summer of 2018, I went to a Dominion Camp Meeting in Columbus, Ohio. Pastor Rod Parsley leads the Camp Meeting at World Harvest Church. When I first got out of jail, after my crossroads with Jesus, I would watch ministers at home on the Christian channels and read my Bible all day. I had no license, and I was hungry! After a powerful encounter with the Holy Spirit, I was hooked to the Presence of God.

Pastor Parsley is a fiery preacher that I would love to hear preach! I love the old-school Pentecostal fire that flows from him. I would see the commercials about a Bible College he has called Valor Christian College, and in my heart, I wanted to attend. At the time, I had no license, my mom had just recently passed, and I was still trying to get in all my hours done for the apprenticeship that I was doing in Cosmetology. The timing was not right, but just because the time is not yet, does not mean it will not be.

Evangelist Levi Lutz, the Director of the Christ for all Nations Evangelism Bootcamp that I attended in Fall 2021 says, "There is a preparatory command and a command of execution." We need to discern the times as the sons of Issachar, men in Israel who knew what Israel should do. A God thing in the wrong timing is not good. We want to walk softly before the Lord as the Holy Spirit leads us.

At the Camp Meeting, I felt the nudge of the Holy Spirit to apply for a scholarship to Valor Christian College. I thought I would continue to serve at my local church in Virginia, continuing to build a clientele at the salon I was working at. I was comfortable, and that was the problem. God will not allow growth in your comfort zone. I received a phone call about receiving a scholarship, but when I would go into prayer, I knew the Lord was nudging me to go be on campus. For the Fall semester, I did not step out in faith because of my "what ifs" and "how" questions. I allowed reasoning to hold me back. I knew deep down, the Lord was stirring the waters, and He wanted me to jump out of the boat.

For months, I remember things just not going right. When you are in obedience, there is a flow and a rhythm that you are in because you are in alignment. When you are in disobedience, all hell could break loose, just to get your tail where you need to be! Now, the longer you walk with God, hopefully that hard knock, becomes more of a gentle nudge to do something because you trust Him more.

I kept questioning God about finances, about who would live with my dad and the list goes on with the reasoning. The Lord laid on my heart that the best place for me to be for my family was and is in the

Father's perfect will. I have heard before that being in the will of God in your life is like a lifeline for your family. After my mom died, I felt an emotional responsibility to support my dad, but sometimes we need to, "Let go and let God." We are not anyone's Savior, and we could be very well in the way of what God wants to do in our family's lives.

I stepped out and relocated to Columbus, Ohio, and am so thankful I did. God provided in miraculous ways, and in that place, the Lord broke the fear of lack off my life. One day, He spoke to my heart, "Jennifer, if you are going to talk about walking by faith, you are going to live it." Again, there are times and seasons. The Apostle Paul was a tentmaker but then he would go out and preach the Gospel. It was during this time in college that He had me not work and fully rely on Him for the first time since I was fifteen years old. I had a poverty mindset that had to be broken, and there was a facet of Him, the Lord being Jehovah

Jireh, our provider, that He wanted to reveal to me during this time.

Bible College is where He broke me down and rebuilt me back up. It was a season of crushing and refining. I know it seemed almost unbearable during those times, but now I am thankful because it built some grit in me before the mission journeys overseas that I have been blessed to encounter. This walk is not always easy, but it is worth it!

God is much more concerned about your internal/spiritual growth than changing your external circumstances. The word refine means "to remove impurities or unwanted elements from (a substance)." The refining fire of the Lord will purge and remove all the mess that we have been holding onto within, but first we must allow Him to. Our Father is a gentleman, and we must first ask, but always know He is willing to form and fashion you into an instrument fit for the master's use.

I am sure Joseph, one of Jacob's twelve sons in the Bible, had questions about what he went through. God gave him a dream that he would rule and his family would bow down to him. Then after sharing this dream, his brothers were jealous and sold him into slavery. He was taken to Egypt and eventually became a servant for Potiphar, one of Pharaoh's officials. Potiphar's wife tried to seduce Joseph, accused him of attempted rape and he was thrown into prison. The Lord was with Joseph and granted him favor in the eyes of the prison warden. Later, Joseph had the opportunity to interpret a dream of Pharoah, and God opened the door for him to be placed in charge of Egypt during a famine.

I share this story because God was doing something in Joseph during the tough times. His pain was not in vain! In fact, it was sharpening him and building character that would sustain the promise. What good is it for God to bless you and launch you into destiny when you do not have the capacity to handle what He blesses you with? He is making you to be a strong pillar, to be able to sustain what He has for you.

There is a responsibility with blessing. Joseph's heart had to remain in a right posture when the brothers that hurt him and were jealous of him now needed his help during a famine in the land. God could trust him to steward the blessing rightly.

Kathryn Kuhlman said that our Father is not looking for gold or silver vessels but willing vessels. He is looking for your yes and cooperation with the Spirit's sanctifying work in your life. Only a Holy God can make men and women Holy. To think that we could try to do something to make us acceptable to God, is to try to rely on self, and Jesus already made a way for us to be right with God. The atoning blood has you covered from the moment that you asked Him into your heart and made Him Lord until you meet Him in Glory. As long as you keep believing in His finished work, you will stay under the umbrella of the shed blood on Calvary. Before you ever said yes to Him, He chose you and has a beautiful purpose for you on the Earth.

8.

Kairos- An Appointed Time

In my third semester in Bible College, I felt the "go" by the Holy Spirit to get a part-time job at a local salon. I also thought this was a good idea because I needed the money! I have learned that we may think what God is asking of us is for one reason in our personal life, but when we are connected to Him through an intimate relationship, the Holy Spirit will lead us places, not at all because of us. He will lead us places, because we are sensitive to the Spirit and what He wants to release in an atmosphere through us. Our assignment could be to go into a place and use the Sword of the Spirit, the Word of God, to break barriers.

We must take our eyes off our needs, and get our mind on spiritual things, things of eternal value. Colossians 3:1-2 says, "Since, then, you have been raised with Christ, set your hearts on things above, where Christ is, seated at the right hand of God. Set your minds on things above, not on earthly things."

I am sharing this with you because I was only at this salon for three months, and then the Lord spoke to my heart to lay it down. I thought to myself, "Well Lord, did I miss you? I thought I had peace in my heart about entering this job." He revealed to me that the job was not about me and showed me that it was about the prayers He was releasing through me while there. He showed me the people that I had worked alongside who were going through some challenging times! Some were experiencing deep loss through unexpected deaths in the family and were trying to navigate through the grief. The Lord used me in this short season to bring hope to hurting hearts. I had my mindset on how short the season had been, but His purposes for me being there were finished.

God is a God of purpose, and there are people and places that He has ordered your steps to come across, but if you are stuck on expired seasons and remaining in a natural mindset of how you think things should be, you will never fulfill the destiny full of faith that He has for you! May we ask the Lord to have the mind of the Spirit, not the mind of the flesh. His way of doing things is always profitable in the Spirit and in the natural.

The week after I obeyed and quit my job, I got a text from Pastor Parsley's armor bearer asking if I could come to learn how to do his hair for *Breakthrough,* his broadcast that airs worldwide. This is the same broadcast I would watch when I was radically saved, and I remember being drawn to that old-school Pentecostal fire! The Scripture Proverbs 18:16 rang in my heart, "A gift opens the way and ushers the giver into the presence of the great." I was in complete awe that God had opened the door to be even in the same room of such a General in the Faith. I would get so nervous just being in Pastor Parsley's presence, but it was my reverential respect for the man of God.

Honor will carry you places, and it is something that this culture in this society lacks. Do not be one who feels entitled but be thankful for the grace of the Lord that carries you. 1 Thessalonians 5:12, "Now we ask you, brothers and sisters to acknowledge those who work hard among you, who care for you in the Lord and who admonish you."

I believe because of the obedience in laying down the job at the salon, the Lord opened the door for me to serve the man of God. Obedience is always better than sacrifice. Flow with the Holy Spirit and watch the Lord open doors no man can shut

(Revelations 3:7). Let God be your doorkeeper and see the miraculous in your life!

A friend had invited me to a women's conference that Judy Jacob's was hosting in her hometown of Cleveland, Tennessee. That weekend of the conference, we had an event at the dorms called "Dorm Wars." For years it has been a tradition of the college for the women and men to decorate each of their dorms, and then have the first family judge which one was decorated best according to the chosen theme. I remember going before the Lord saying, "Lord, I know that you want me to go to this women's conference, but we have 'Dorm Wars,' and while being in leadership, I don't know if that is going to look well me leaving out of state."

To the natural mind, it looked like it would be foolish, but the Spirit of God led me to get me where I needed to be. Not long after going before the Lord in prayer, it turned out, "Dorm Wars" got cancelled for the first time in years. I knew this was more of a seal of approval I needed to get to this conference. I remember there was so much resistance before getting to Tennessee, but now I realize why, because this encounter changed the course of my life.

  While in school, pastors and professors would tell me, "You need someone to pour into you, you need a spiritual mother/mentor." Deep down, I knew I needed someone to be accountable to. Yes, I was accountable to the Lord, but I desired to go deeper in my walk and desired someone to pour into me. I knew better than to try to pick someone for that role in my life. It must be someone ordained by the Lord. I was pouring out so much to the young ladies in the dorms, and I was feeling dry. If we ever feel we are getting to a place of feeling dry, we need to go to the source. Jesus is the well that will never run dry, and we do not have to be in a state of dryness. I did not know what I needed, but God did, exceeding my expectations.

The third day while I was at this women's conference, this woman named Laura Crocker, with bright red hair and big blue eyes came bouncing over with a huge smile. She started speaking with me and began to tell me how she did jail ministry, and immediately, I began sharing with her how I radically surrendered to Jesus while in jail in 2013. I remember there was such a stirring in my spirit after speaking with her. I went to sit down, then she brought over a ministry card with her number. She asked me if I would record my testimony to share with the ladies in recovery at her ministry home.

Right after we had met, Karen Wheaton was the speaker who preached the next session in the conference. Her sermon was titled, "KAIROS." In the Greek, Kairos means appointed times where everything begins to shift. Indeed, my whole life was about to shift. We kept in contact, began praying on the phone and it amazed me how I would be thinking about something, and she would pray exactly what was concerning me. God had already knit us together by the Spirit. I never knew how detailed God is in relationships until I met her. God knew I had a void in my life from my natural mother passing, and though she loved me much, she was very broken and loved me as she knew how to in her brokenness.

The conference we attended was in November of 2019, and by December, I felt the nudge of the Lord to go to Alabama to visit her women's ministry. During our winter break, we had two weeks off from campus. I was led to visit family in Virginia for Christmas for a week, then headed to Alabama to spend a week at Mama Laura's ministry called "Awakening the Bride." I did not know what it all meant, and truthfully, it looked a little crazy. I had never been to Alabama and had just met this lady but knew there was such a strong unction in my spirit to go. After I agreed to go on the trip, the Holy Spirit spoke to my heart that an impartation would be needed for the girls I was leading in my quad in the dorms; there would be something deposited for this next season of leadership in my life.

Sometimes it is only after we agree and say yes to the command of the Lord, that He begins to share more details. Even if He does not, be like Mary, Jesus' mother, at the first miracle of turning the water into wine in Cana, "Just do what He says." We must get to a place where we do not need any sign, no other detail, other than the Word of the Lord. And again, this all comes as you are growing with the Father, you begin to know His character. Trust comes with getting to know someone. The more time you spend with them, the more you can trust.

Prayer to see the Lord Rightly

Father, I come to you asking you to help me to see you rightly.

I repent of allowing guilt and shame to hinder your love.

I ask you help me to trust you as a loving Father,

I ask you to pour your tangible love into every crevice of my being.

Give me eyes to see your goodness and majesty in my life,

And may I always run to your embrace and never away.

In Jesus' name,

Amen.

9.

Get Ready to Shift

I obeyed the Holy Spirit and drove from Virginia to Alabama in the Winter of 2019. It was so funny, because the night before I left, I had been at my dad's house, and he decided to put on the movie *Forrest Gump.* He was joking and said, "Jenny is going to Alabama!" It was heartwarming in the sense that I knew that my Abba Father had led me to go, but then my father who raised me was speaking in the natural to confirm the "Go ahead!"

I was driving down the road of Mama Laura's ministry, and these thoughts began to come, "What are you doing? You do not even know this lady. This is crazy! You drove all the way here…!" All this nonsense started bombarding my mind, and you know what I did? I pressed on!

Have you noticed when you are about to step into something new or about to have a breakthrough, how the enemy at times, can try to discourage you by injecting thoughts into your mind to try to get you off course? When that happens, you should know you are on your way to another Glory. Keep pressing, keep persevering toward the mark. It is not about how well we start but how we finish. We cannot get caught up in this world's entanglements or allow our minds' reasoning to talk us out of what our spirit man knows to be true.

When I finally got onto the ministry's grounds, I felt the Glory of God upon the land. It was so heavy! I was welcomed by Mama Laura, her daughter Laurie and a young lady named Felicia who had been in the program there. The love that I encountered was so beautiful. When they wrapped their arms around me,

I began to weep. My spirit man knew that this house of Glory would be a divine place for me. I did not know when, but my spirit man knew I would one day live in this place.

At first, I did not know how to act around Mama Laura. She reassured me every night as we would worship, pray, and share our hearts, that she was for me, and wanted nothing from me but to love me. I had been a Christian for quite some time now, but the love she extended revealed some places that still needed healing. I still had some walls up and honestly thought this lady was too good to be true.

Before meeting Mama Laura, I knew I was called to the ministry, and I loved Jesus, but I do not believe I allowed Him or other people to love me how they could fully. Past relationships had so wounded me, that I had been closed off on the receiving end. I gave out love but still had some guard up myself. Not only that, but I dealt with a spirit of rejection from the womb and dealt with an orphan spirit, never feeling as if I belonged.

Mama Laura was so gentle and kind. She truly is a conduit of the Lord's love and grace. Later, I discovered that her daughter Laurie had a dream about Mama Laura a week before we met. In the dream, they were at a restaurant, and Mama was so big and pregnant. She said everyone was saying in the dream, "You are so big."

The Lord was preparing her heart for me being engrafted into the family. Also, Mama Laura had been prophesied over that she would have twins. It turns out Laurie and I were both born in December 1988. In 1988 is when Mama Laura surrendered to the Lord and got filled with the Holy Ghost! How good is our God? We truly were children birthed by the Spirit! You may feel like you have missed out on a certain area in your life, but if you turn to the Lord, He will be sure to restore you. He is a faithful Father.

Not only did I visit Mama Laura while in Alabama, but it also turned out my Great Aunt Carol lived in the next county over. I had not seen her in years. It was so precious because when my natural mother was pregnant, my Great Aunt Carol housed her and helped her through her pregnancy. When I was visiting her, I saw a painting of a man who was writing. My spirit man leaped when I saw him. Aunt Carol was so funny. She approached me and said, "That is the man in the Bible who wrote the Bible while he was in prison." I said, "You mean the Apostle Paul?" She said, "Oh yeah, that is him." I immediately fell in love with this painting and the frame around it. She turned to it, then turned to me, and asked if I wanted it. One of her friends had passed into Glory, and her family had passed the painting to my Great Aunt Carol. I gladly accepted the gift.

When I look at this painting, I am reminded of how grounded in the Lord the Apostle Paul was even in the midst of hardship. Everything around us can be shaken, but we can remain steadfast internally as we are built on a solid foundation, Jesus, the chief cornerstone. I debated whether I should take this elaborate painting to my college dorm. I was concerned that it might get messed up, but it was so gorgeous! I could not help but bring it with me.

Even though Christmas had passed, Mama Laura and Laurie went all out lavishing me with gifts. I was so overwhelmed with the love that they were showing me, even though we had not known each other long. The faithfulness of our Father in Heaven had brought these two ladies into my life to be examples of His love for me. Appreciate the people that the Father places in your life to express His great love for you and you to them.

As I packed up my car after coming to visit Alabama, I realized that I had gone to another level in my walk with the Lord. I had undoubtedly hit another realm of Glory. I remember when I was there for New Year's, we went to their Pastor's house to celebrate. We were all wrecked in the Holy Spirit, laughing hysterically. I was surrounded by people who knew how to swim in the river of God. It was bittersweet leaving Alabama, but I knew deep down I would be back. With my car loaded down with gifts and, more importantly, loaded with spiritual blessings within, I drove back to Ohio. I was overwhelmed by how good the Lord and He had been to me during this trip.

While driving back to Columbus, Ohio, I stopped to get some gas in Knoxville, Tennessee. There was a homeless gentleman outside of the gas station. The Holy Spirit had unctioned me to speak to the man outside as I was in the restroom. As I approached him, I realized this African American man had the bluest eyes I had ever seen. I began to ask him what his name was, and he said his name was

"Life." I had never met a man named "Life" before. He began telling me he did not choose to be homeless but was waiting on his disability check and told me how he fell into tough times after his mother had passed. I began to leave, thinking I had a long way to go before I got back to campus, and I had a service that Wednesday night that I wanted to attend. The Holy Spirit convicted me, and He spoke to my heart to minister more to the man. Then I went across the street to get him some food.

The first Sunday back at World Harvest Church after I returned to Columbus from Winter break, we had a guest preacher from the Bronx. The name of his sermon "There is Life." My mouth dropped wide open. Then he began preaching out of Acts and saying he was about to preach on his favorite person in the Bible, apart from Jesus. I knew before he spoke the name that he was referring to the Apostle Paul. This amazed me because as I journeyed back to campus, I had the beautiful painting that was given to me, the painting of the Apostle Paul, in my car while I met a man named Life.

I still to this day believe that he was an angel, and the Lord wanted to see if I would be obedient to stop for him. We must not be so quick to get to the next place when our assignment is to first be in tune with the Lord. If I had missed the leading of the Spirit, I would have missed this amazing encounter. It showed me how every detail of our lives is in His hands and how He desires us to walk in a supernatural flow in every area of our lives.

When I returned to the dorms, my leader noticed a complete difference in me. Not only was there much impartation on my trip to Alabama, but the love and healing that I received made me walk more in my position of authority as a daughter of the King. Having that motherly love and covering took me to another place in my identity as a daughter. I now felt a security that I had not known before. I recognized such a change within myself. It is easier to see change in others, but for ourselves, it may take a little while to see the transformation. I saw it in this case, and boy, I felt it!

10.

Don't Miss Your Moment

Three months had passed since I returned to campus from Alabama, and now it was Spring break. I had been preparing for a trip to Virginia when one of my dorm friends came to my room. She and I prayed and worshipped most of the night. Little did I know this would be my last night living in the dorms. I drove to Virginia, and then while I was on break, the covid outbreak happened.

The day I was supposed to leave to drive back to Columbus, I felt a restraint in my spirit, which was a red light to halt. I ended up staying at my Dad's an extra day, and then I received a message from the

Dean of Students that we were not to return to campus and, if we had, we must head back home.

I honestly did not understand why I felt that restraint in my spirit, but the Holy Ghost did. This is another example of when you have a check in your spirit, you do not need to know the answers, but heed it! Later you may find out why you had the check, but even if the Lord does not reveal it, heeding is always best to avoid consequences.

After being home for a few weeks, I read my Bible while staying at my aunt and uncle's house when the Holy Spirit spoke to my heart and said, "Go to Alabama. Do not miss your moment." I did not understand what this meant, although I realized that most everything was beginning to shut down due to the covid outbreak. The news said you must only drive if absolutely necessary. I packed up my stuff and did not even tell most of my family in Virginia that I was driving to Alabama. I knew if I told them before I left, they would try to persuade me to stay in Virginia and that leaving would not be safe. I know that being in the Father's perfect will is where true safety resides, so I obeyed.

I drove through this horrible storm down to Alabama, but I had such peace in my spirit, knowing this was the leading of the Lord. When I finally got there, my Mama Laura ran out and hugged me as she helped me get my things into her place. I felt safe. I felt at home. Little did I know this would be the beginning of a pivotal time of inner healing and growing in the Glory of the Lord.

Mama Laura was and is unlike anyone I had ever met. I remember thinking to myself, "This lady never changes." She is steadfast and does not move off the Word of God. If anything would be troubling me, or if I had a question, she would and still always leads me to, "What does the Word say?" She taught me what it was to sit and wait upon the Lord in the Glory.

I knew about God for years and had many power encounters with the Holy Spirit. As a Christian, you do not get saved and never need fresh infillings of the Holy Ghost. It is a lifelong journey of repentance and refreshing of the Spirit. As we wait upon the Lord, He will pour new oil upon our life.

Mama Laura practiced lying prostrate before the Lord for exceptionally lengthy periods. I had seen where people would be in worship and would do this as a sign of reverence, but I had not quite seen someone do it in the way she would. At her ministry, Awakening the Bride, I learned the discipline of waiting upon the Glory, the manifest Presence of the Lord.

One day as I was lying prostrate, the Holy Spirit began to speak to me about Him being in the "Low place." I began to hear Him and see visions more clearly as I waited for the weight of His Glory. We must wait on the weight. There is a place in the Lord where we are still before Him, where there is no amount of human effort, but just waiting upon the Lord to deposit as He wants. The Bible says in Zechariah 4:6, "It is not by might, it is not my power, but by His Spirit." When we humble ourselves before Him, He can do what only He can do.

There have been moments in my life where I would seek the Lord in a situation and ask Him to speak or give me a Scripture. I would then have a leading by peace to rest physically from all my "trying to get something." As I obeyed to rest from striving, I would have a vision or even a dream of the answer I was trying so hard to get an answer to.

There had been a big eighteen-wheeler parked down the street from us in Alabama for an extended period of time. On the side of the truck was a picture of a young boy lying on a mattress, so content. As I walked by it one day, the Lord said, "Child-like faith brings the rest."

Sometimes, we over-complicate spiritual things. God can speak to us in many ways if our spiritual eyes are open. Just as much as we have five physical senses in the natural world, we also have those senses in the spiritual realm. Ask for the Lord to awaken you to see Him in new and fresh ways. When we seek the Lord first and allow His Presence room in us, it can make the everyday mundane acts of life enjoyable.

While in Alabama during the lockdown, I met some of the most amazing people who knew what it was to abide in the river of the Holy Spirit. I barely knew them, but I knew in my spirit they were my people! I cannot tell you how much of the love of the Father poured through them and helped me grow in this season.

One night while at Mama's ministry, I dreamed that I was cleaning my dorm room out at Valor Bible College. There was another young lady who had been cleaning hers out too. When I awoke, I asked the Lord why I had been cleaning my dorm room when I still had another semester until graduation. Then, it all dawned on me that when I was in the dorms, one young lady who had been the one in my dream asked me what my plans were after graduating. I told her I would stay a third year and get a second degree. She whipped her head around so fast and began to say, "What if that is not what God has?" I was shocked she was so bold to say this with such conviction, being that I was secure in where God had me. He had been doing so much and opening so many doors; why would He want me to leave? I pondered.

The following day after I had this dream, I was in the restroom getting ready, and the Lord spoke to my heart, "Jennifer, remember when you delayed getting to Bible College a semester because of the fear of the unknown? Now I have redeemed the time and have taken you to the next part of your journey. Finish the last semester online." I was in awe at how the Lord had worked everything out. He is so into the details, and even if we get off track, He is so good at working ALL things together for our good, because we love Him and are called according to His purposes (Romans 8:28).

Stay encouraged if you feel that you have veered off the path. The Holy Spirit is the best guide and can get you on the right path if you are still and obey. Also, when the Lord says GO, trust His way is the best way!

11.

The Supernatural Hand of God

While living in Alabama, I saw my Mama Laura's walk of faith and how the Lord, as a faithful Father, delighted to provide for every need. Two ministry buildings were supernaturally given to her. After years of jail ministry, the Lord had given her the vision to have a home with women who had just gotten out of jail and were transitioning back into the world. I know just how vital this is. Your environments matter, and especially as a new believer, you need people around you who are discipling you in the things of God.

The Lord told Mama Laura to believe for the building, not pay for the building. The Lord wants to give us divine instruction as we believe for a thing instead of us rushing into the arm of the flesh. Through Christ, we can be blessed receivers of all that we need. Mama would say whenever there was a need, "Let's pray and believe God for it."

For a few years, the Lord had laid on my heart that I would have a hair salon and do ministry out of it. I did not know how it would come to pass, but I kept it alive in my heart. While I was in Bible College, I called Mama Laura one night, and one of the ladies from her ministry had drawn a picture of a crown with the word Glory over it. They had been in worship, and the Holy Spirit dropped in her spirit to draw it. Little did this young lady know I had been praying and believing for a future salon called "Crown of Glory Hair." My heart was so full of expectancy!

After moving to Alabama, Mama and I believed for the future salon. One day she came to me and asked if I would want to use one of the rooms out of one of the ministry buildings. Honestly, I did not even know that it was an option, but I was thrilled at the idea. I decided to go for it, and I testify God supplied every need in that salon: the chairs, the lighting, the shampoo sink, the tools, and all the décor. We had gone down to the neighbor who was a carpenter and asked him to make my shelves for my hair color and supplies. When he came to deliver it, he said, "It is on me!"

This season in Alabama showed me how the Lord wants to care for His children. I also realize that there is seed time and harvest. For years my Daddy would say, "Jennifer, you give all of your money to the church, and you don't even have much." I had put much seed in the ground and saw the harvest being returned. No seed equals no harvest!

One year into Bible College, I had been T-boned in an accident by an unlicensed driver. I was unfamiliar with this new intersection and had proceeded, thinking it was a four-way stop. I flipped my SUV twice and landed on my tires. I was shaken to my core! I remember a man rushed up to see if I was okay. As he kept talking, I was not able to say a word. I knew that I had divine assistance during that wreck. There is no way that I would have been able to survive without it! For a while after, I would think about the wreck and weep before the Lord. I remembered as my car was flipping, gripping the wheel, and bracing myself, thinking, "This is it."

The following Sunday, I got a message from a lady at church asking if I would be in service. After the service, she pulled me aside and said she and her husband were discussing my accident. They thought that I could have her old Acura. Her husband had been seeing my journey with the Lord on Facebook, and he saw how my life was transformed. He had lived in the town where I graduated High School, meaning he knew the alcoholic, wild-party girl I was before surrendering to Christ. Now, he had seen me serving and loving Jesus with all I had. I was utterly amazed that in less than twenty-four hours, the Lord had provided me a car to return to Bible College with after break.

    The Lord wants to provide for His children. Genesis 50:20 says what the enemy meant for harm God will turn it around if we will just trust Him. Since I was 15 years old, I have worked a job, sometimes two jobs to provide, and since surrendering full-heartedly to the Lord in 2013, there are times when the Lord has had to help me to trust in the area of finances. Growing up, my parents argued much over finances, and honestly, the fear of lack had to be severed. Romans 1:17 says, "The just shall live by faith." The Lord wants us to become like children, completely reliant on Him for ALL things.

12.

Way Maker

During the covid lockdown, I remember seeing a friend of mine, Urmi, from Bible College's journey on Facebook. She had attended the Christ for all Nations Evangelism Bootcamp in Orlando, Florida. She was more reserved in college, but when we got alone to pray, she was always filled with wisdom and super passionate. Seeing her journey through the Bootcamp was a blessing to see her truly come out of her shell. I knew deep down that I would love to do something like that one day.

It had been months since the previous Bootcamp had graduated when Mama Laura came to tell me that she had just received an email from Christ for all Nations stating that applications were now open for the next training. I did not even have to pray because I knew how my spirit bore witness that this was a green light to "GO." Of course, seek the Lord and His counsel for your life in all things, but when your spirit bears witness, follow peace!

While I was in Bible college, Mama Laura had a dream about me on a steam engine while I was laughing. The Lord spoke in the dream, "The old ways are the fast track." When I read the email from the Bootcamp, it said, "The fast track to the mission field!"

I applied for the Bootcamp, and I checked my email every day. I was in such anticipation. I remember my times in jail, when I would have visions of mass crusades, not knowing that the sea of people I would see as I worshipped the Lord was a crusade. I absolutely had no idea how the Lord would do it through me and how He would get me to it. The Bootcamp was the vehicle He chose to launch me into this part of His calling for my life.

The Lord is so beautiful and so merciful that even in my being imprisoned in the natural, He was revealing to me good plans and purposes He had for my life. No matter where you may find yourself, when you look to the Lord, He wants to speak life over you. John 10:10 says that the Lord has come to give us life abundantly.

About a month after I applied for the training, Mama Laura, my sister Laurie, and I visited one of Mama's friends from Oral Roberts University. One night while there, I laid prostrate before the Lord and said, "I must have more of you, God. Whatever it takes!"

As I write, I think of 1 Samuel 1, when Hannah cries out for a son. Peninnah, her husband Elkanah's other wife, provoked her to desperation in prayer.

Hannah vows to offer her son to the Lord, and the Lord opens her womb. The Lord responds in our distress!

The very next day, after I laid before the Lord in prayer, I got a call from a gentleman named Abraham from the second Bootcamp. He left a message that I had been accepted into the next phase of the application process. Now, the interview was to be scheduled via Zoom. After receiving that call, I fell to my knees and cried out to the Lord in thankfulness. Everything within me knew this was the next step in my journey with the Lord. My sweet sister Laurie ran to her checkbook and sowed the first seed of $333 for the training.

After my interview with CfaN, they told me they would get back to me in a week or so. I received word the very next day that I had been accepted! Oh, the joy and excitement that flooded my being! I was one of the last people to be accepted, being it was so close to the day of Orientation. I had three and ½ weeks to come up with $4000 for the training due within days of being accepted. There were previous due dates in increments, but because of the late acceptance, this is why it had all been due. This was stretching my faith! Faith is like a muscle; if you do not use it, it will not grow. Plus, believing God is fun because you get to see Him do what He can do. Nothing shall be impossible with Him! (Luke 1:37).

My Mama and I discussed the $4,000 that was due, and she said, "We are going to pray and believe for all of it to come in today!" We prayed in the Holy Ghost, and she got a call minutes later! It was a couple that we went to church with. They told my Mama they wanted to get a check into my hands for the training. She graciously told them we would get it from them on Wednesday at Bible Study. They insisted on bringing it to us that night after we ministered at the local jail. The Lord laid it on their hearts to get it to me so I would have it in on the due date! They drove counties away with their newborn baby in the rain to get me this card. As we left the jail, they approached me with a card with a check in it. The check was $4,500! I could not believe my eyes for a moment. My God showed me His faithfulness and in a quickness!

I left that parking lot of the jail in awe of the goodness of the Lord. I said in my heart, "Lord, forgive me for ever doubting your faithfulness." The following day, I got all of the $4000 in on time and put the remaining $500 towards our Initiation trip in Africa. Just wait, it gets better! I still needed funds for accommodations while in Orlando. About a week later, I had $2000 that popped into my bank account. I thought this was a glitch with my bank, but the $2000 never left my account as time passed. The Lord supernaturally provided for me to have funds to look for accommodations! We serve a limitless God!

Later in the training, Mama and I had been praying for $315 to pay off my Bootcamp Graduation ring and Dog Tag. As Mama usually says, "We will believe God for it." The following day, I felt led to check my business account from the salon in Alabama. I kept this account open because I still needed to pay my taxes for that year. Although, throughout the training, I had not deposited, nor had I withdrawn, any money in this account. I checked it, and to my surprise, I had $330 extra in my account. Once I saw the balance, the Lord spoke to my heart, "When you take care of my business, I will always take care of your business." One of the Scriptures that the Lord had on my heart to pray into during the training was John 3:30, "He must increase, but I must decrease," then, this is the amount He drops into my account! When I look at my Bootcamp class ring, I know that my Beloved Bridegroom King paid for it! How beautiful!

13.

Another Shift

Halfway through the Bootcamp, the Lord had been stirring a desire to move to Orlando after the training. When I had left Alabama, I had no idea that He was shifting me altogether and that Orlando would now be my home base. From a natural perspective, it does not make much sense when things are going well in a particular place why the Lord would shift you to another location. There are times and seasons, and when an assignment is through, you must be like the wind being able to shift to another direction.

Our life is not our own, and the Lord has prepared in advance good works before the very foundation of the Earth for us to walk out (Ephesians 2:10). These good works are in Christ Jesus. Your position in Him, as a born-again believer, is secure. When we are born again, we have the precious Holy Spirit, a seal of our inheritance, to lead and guide us into these works.

I remember the very day that the Lord encountered me and solidified Him leading me in the move. I was reading Daniel Kolenda's *Live Before You Die*, and I was reading about how God's will is not challenging to figure out. Evangelist Daniel talks about a group of people out in the desert who were studying cacti. They had run out of water in the middle of nowhere. Then, some of the people saw a pool of water with a palm tree over it. The more skilled experimenter thought to himself, "This is a mirage; it cannot truly be there." When the other less skilled experimenters decided they would run to the pool of water, they discovered it was not a mirage but an actual body of water. The more experienced man ended up dying because he thought it was too good to be true, while the others who believed the water was there had their thirst quenched.

How often is it like that with believers? We become intimately acquainted with the Lord in the vastness of His mercy and love in the beginning phases of our journey with Christ. Then over time, we can overcomplicate and over-spiritualize things to the point that what was right in our faces now seems so far away because of much overthinking. In speaking, that seems easy, but when you make Jesus Lord and sincerely ask for His guidance, He will not leave you hanging.

It delights our Father's heart when we seek His plans for us, as He is watching them unfold. Proverbs 25:2 says, "It is the glory of God to conceal a matter; to search out a matter is the glory of kings." The one who breathed life into dust, forming human beings out of His words, can surely be trusted with your precious life. He has a good track record, not failing yet, and never will. That is our God!

The wild thing about this day is that as I was reading *Live Before You Die*, I sat beside a pool of water with palm trees surrounding it. There is only a little downtime during the Bootcamp training, which is on purpose. It is meant to push you to your limits so that there is a deeper level of dependency on the Lord. Sitting by the pool of water, reading this very chapter at that moment, I felt the alignment of Heaven.

Have you ever been in a particular place where everything within you, spirit, soul, and body, feels like you are in an "AHA," moment? I like to call an "AHA," moment one of those times where you feel the significance of the Scripture Psalm 37:23, "The Lord makes firm the steps of the one who delights in him." In these moments, you know you are in the right place at the right time, on the path the Lord has set before you.

There is no greater feeling to me than knowing I am in step with what the Lord has for me. My heart's cry is to hear those words, "Well done, good and faithful servant." At the end of my life on Earth, may the assignments that He has me to fulfill for His Glory be accomplished by His grace, and I pray that for you as well.

The Holy Spirit so engulfed me that I felt like waves of electricity going through my body as I read the pages on finding the will of God. I paused momentarily and closed my eyes to take it all in. I heard the Lord say, "I am relocating you to this place." For weeks, I had the desire to stay after the training, but now I knew that this was indeed the Lord giving me that desire.

The next day I served at the new to Nation's tent, which Nations Church is the local church expression of CfaN. This man comes up to me, who I barely know, and says, "What are you doing after Bootcamp?" I looked at him strangely because I knew the radical encounter I had with the Holy Spirit the day before. I told him I believed I would stay in Orlando, and I was not sure how the Lord would do it, but He would make a way. He began to testify on how the Lord had provided the previous seven months for him and his children all by faith.

Just wait, it gets better! Another lady who worked for Nations Church approached me and said, "I feel like you are our people. You belong here." I began to tell her how the Lord had been speaking to me about relocating, how the Lord had provided a hair salon supernaturally at the ministry I was at in Alabama, and how now, He was speaking to lay it all down. She began prophesying about the move, and my spirit man was running! The hope and peace of the Lord was astounding. I knew my God was up to something. I did not know what it all looked like, and to be honest, I still do not understand what it all looks like, but I do know that He is the master builder. We can trust Him with every piece of the puzzle, knowing He cares for us and has our absolute best interests at heart.

The salon I had in Alabama was called "Crown of Glory." Mind you, when the Lord spoke to me about laying it all down at His feet, I was driving past a church down the street from our church called "Crown of Glory." As I was passing the church, the song by Stephanie Gretzinger came on, "All is for your Glory." She talks about how all man's vain and high ambitions will be brought low. So many interweavings of Him, divinely speaking. I knew in my heart the Lord was speaking to me about just letting it all go. We are stewards of all that the Lord gives in this life. If He says lay it down, obedience is necessary.

Later that night, as I was at Jesus Image, Michael Koulianos spoke on Abraham and how he was willing to sacrifice the promise, his beloved Isaac, for the sake of obeying the Lord. Confirmation after confirmation, it had been settled; Orlando would be home.

In my heart, I thought to myself, "Lord, I know you are calling me to move, but you did just give me a family to run in ministry with." Little did I know what was around the corner. I shared with Mama Laura what the Lord was revealing to me, and she confirmed that when I left for Bootcamp, the Lord told her that I would be staying in Orlando. I have learned many things from her, but one is knowing when or if to say something the Lord reveals. There are words the Lord has given her concerning me, but when the Lord releases, she will tell me. The Lord wants us to know His voice and hear it from Him first. Prophecies should always confirm what has already been revealed from the Father. Sometimes the Lord will reveal something because He trusts us to pray about a matter, and nothing is to be said. Lord, help us be sensitive when you reveal something so that we steward it rightly!

After much prayer, to my surprise, Mama Laura told me that the Lord spoke to her about moving to Florida and told her to get in a position to help me. I did not even know what the Lord was moving me to Orlando for, and He was also speaking to her about it. To say I was excited would be a complete understatement. She, Laurie, and I would be journeying into this next season to a new region together as a family.

Not long after the Lord spoke to her about moving, she went to church, and our Pastor started prophesying to the church, "If you are in your fifties and the Lord tells you to shift, what are you going to do?" There was so much she said that day that confirmed the Lord was also moving Mama Laura.

Then there had been word that Pastor Nassan was in town from Uganda. He was a Pastor/friend who came up under the same ministry Mama used to serve under. She pulled up to the church, and there were palm trees in front of the church in Alabama. The first church I had ever heard of that had palm trees in Alabama! The church he was speaking at was called "New Beginnings." She gets into the service, and he first says, "Are you happy?" And if you know the ministry of Christ for all Nations, the founder, Evangelist Bonnke, would say this very phrase quite often. Pastor Nassan says, "You may be a woman, but you can drive a big 18-wheeler." The Lord was making it clear that Florida was our next.

For months, Mama would look for a place for us to relocate to in the Orlando area, but to no avail, found nothing. I told her I felt in my spirit that something would open up for us when we all three visited the Jesus 21' Conference and stepped on the soil together. That is precisely what happened! We got there, and it turned out one of the realtors Mama spoke with was managing some duplexes. A tree fell on one of the duplexes, pushing the couple to move sooner into the new house they were building. Praise God they were not hurt, but now they would renovate the duplex, and it would be ready in the next month for new residents to move in. It had three bedrooms and a fenced-in backyard for our dogs. It was truly divine! I was ecstatic about the upcoming move. When I returned from Bootcamp, I knew the grace had been lifted to stay in Alabama. I was in Alabama, but my heart was in Orlando.

  I remember visiting family in Virginia after graduating from Bootcamp around the holidays. After visiting my home church, formally the Bridge Church, which is now City Reach, one of the elders in the church invited me to eat lunch with her after the service. As we ate pancakes at IHOP, I shared all the marvelous things the Lord did while at Bootcamp and our Initiation trip in Nigeria, Africa. I began to tell her how the Lord was leading me to move to Orlando and how it did not make any logical sense to the mind. The joy of the Lord came upon us, and neither of us could stop laughing. I felt the Holy Ghost's nudge to ask our server if we could pray for her. I asked the young lady, "Ma'am, what is your name?" She looked back at me from the register and said, "Sherlando, like Orlando." My mouth dropped as I looked over at Ms. Betty. The Lord does have a sense of humor! Sherlando told us that she was named after her father, Orlando. Her mother had just passed months before and needed help coping with her being gone.

We prayed, and I walked out that IHOP supercharged, knowing that the Spirit of the living

God had me rightly aligned with what He has for my life. How amazing it is that the Spirit nudged me to be a blessing and pray for this young lady, and in turn, she blessed me without even realizing it. The Lord has a way of taking care of ALL ends. He is truly a great God.

14.

He is the Door

While we were waiting to move to Orlando, I dreamed I was at a table with a couple of the leaders from the Bootcamp and had been working with them. I just tucked this dream away in my heart and said, "Lord, if this is a door you have for me, you will open it." Jesus is the door to all things. Matthew 6:33 says, "Seek His kingdom and His righteousness, and all these things will be added to you." We must avoid seeking opportunities and looking for doors of preference. When we seek the Lord to know Him, not to get anything from Him, but to be intimately acquainted with Him, He opens the doors. Presence over presents, always!

The Lord promotes, not man. When the time is right, the Lord will elevate you to the place He has for you, but before that time comes, there is a place of stripping where all the motives are purified. The anointing will take you places, but your character will sustain you. As you place your life as a living sacrifice on the altar, let the fire of God burn every impurity.

The ways of the Kingdom of God are quite contradictory in theory, but the way up is indeed down. This way of lowly living does not ever stop either. It increases as the Spirit leads to promotion; the lower you must go. The accolades, the applause of men, the followings on social media, none of this impresses the Lord. What impresses God is a heart sold out to Him in lovesick abandonment. His most valued treasure is man, who was made in His very own image, and when the Lord entrusts His children to you to be in any leadership, we must manage it not be in a fit. We need to know our lane, what the Lord has called us to, and run in that vein.

We are not called to be cookie-cutter Christians, all doing the same thing. Seek the face of God, and He will reveal to you the purposes and plans He has for you. Do not get weary and run down trying to wear someone else's shoes. Find your fit, then run in the grace and favor of the Lord!

The time had come when the duplex we were moving to was renovated and ready. We rented a giant Penske truck one weekend in January 2022. A massive snowstorm was coming, and we had to move fast. We packed that truck so quickly; I could hardly believe it. We knew we had to get moving quickly, or we may have gotten snowed in. We packed what was needed and left the rest in the ministry buildings to take care of later. Not just because of the bad weather, I also felt so impressed with my whole being that we had to go without delay with the timing of the shift.

As we traveled through the night, Mama Laura drove this big, loaded-down Penske truck. This caused us to be reminded of Pastor Nassan's words, "You may be a little woman, but you can drive a big 18-wheeler!" This was that word! I will never forget how the wind was that night. In my heart, though, I had such expectancy and excitement about this new adventure we were going on with Jesus. I had gotten to a rest stop on the highway, and a little piece of paper fell out of my car out of nowhere. It had been a couple of months since I had seen it. It was a name tag with my name, "Jennifer Whitaker," which my coach in the Bootcamp, Jacqui Ford, had written when she prepared dinner for us. The Lord spoke to my heart, "I have prepared a place for you at the table."

We finally arrived at our new place in Casselberry, Florida. It was definitely a smaller place than we were previously in, but it was cozy! A perfect place for our transition to Florida.

15.

Unexpected Surprises

Not long after we got situated in Orlando, I had the opportunity to do youth crusades in Rwanda, Africa. The goal between the teams on the ground was 500,000 souls won to Jesus. Before the Bootcamp, hearing these numbers would have been hard to grasp. Even in faith, I had not witnessed a catch of fish like this before. Being under the ministry of Evangelist Reinhard Bonnke and now his successor, Evangelist Daniel Kolenda, my faith in the miraculous has increased. The Lord has used CfaN as the vehicle to get me, and countless other evangelists worldwide, to where we need to be, while multiplying and collaborating for the sake of the end-time harvest.

In 1984 in Soweto, South Africa, Kenneth Copeland prophesied that Reinhard would one day preach to millions. In November 2000, this prophecy was fulfilled in Lagos, Nigeria, when 1,093,475 people received Jesus as their Lord and Savior on the final night! The Holy Spirit spoke to Reinhard's heart that he would "plunder hell and populate heaven for Calvary's sake." That is surely what he did during his lifetime, winning nearly 80 million souls to Jesus. Now there is a legacy of Holy Spirit Evangelists being raised up through Christ for all Nations aiming to hit the 150 million mark of souls within this "Decade of Double Harvest," God's vision God has given Evangelist Kolenda during this time.

The Bootcamp training was pivotal in my walk with the Lord. I became even more in love with Jesus and saw how He uses ordinary people, like you and me, to be conduits of His power to the masses and the one. It was wild because years prior to going to Bible College, I had been driving to a salon I had worked at and had been praying in the Holy Ghost. I just felt there was more in store and had gotten to a place where I felt stagnant. I was doing all the right things, but there was no faith in action. Then I passed a vehicle with a license plate that said, "Africa" on it. The weighty Glory of God filled my car. I knew the Lord was going to send me to Africa. At the time, I had no passport but had such a realization that the Lord would do it. Later that week, a whole family from South Africa came into the salon in the small country county of Powhatan. Coincidence? I think not!

The first country in Africa I had the honor to venture to was Nigeria for our Initiation trip. It truly was remarkable! We saw limbs healed, people coming out of wheelchairs, blind eyes restored, and countless other healings! We saw 239,903 salvations during the Initiation between all of our teams! It was like the book of Acts before my eyes, and this is a way of life everywhere these evangelists go. Matthew 10:8 says, "Heal the sick, cleanse the lepers, raise the dead, cast out demons. Freely you have received, freely give." The people, even more than that, family, I have gained from CfaN, Nations, and the Bootcamp have been so dear to my heart. I am forever grateful to the Lord for finding a people of laid-down lovers, radical in the pursuit of plundering hell and populating Heaven!

As I flew into Rwanda to do youth crusades, a lady named Faith administered my covid test. I looked down at my receipt, which said, "Received by Faith." Later, when I needed an African phone, the lady connecting my line, her name was Joy. I thought, "Lord, I am expectant of what you are about to do!"

One day after our team had gotten out of a youth crusade, some of my fellow evangelist friends said, "We should do a Gospel Crusade here." One evangelist with us had been to Rwanda multiple times and had some connections to some Pastors. We met with one of them, but he was somewhat apprehensive because the government still did not allow large gatherings due to covid; even the churches could only allow a certain amount of people in.

Eventually, after sharing the vision of churches coming together in unity, having the Gospel Crusade, and how it would bring more people into the church since the decline after covid, the Pastor agreed to help. At first, they talked to the government, and they said we could have a large gathering of a certain number of people. Then a couple of days later, they opened all of Rwanda for crusades, and churches were open to full capacity! I was in awe of the Lord!

I truly knew God wanted to do something special in this region.

One of the most popular Gospel music artists from Rwamagana, where we held the crusade, was on board to help with worship. Then a man who set up platforms for the president gave us a huge deal on the stage. I will not say that we did not come up against some hurdles along the way while trying to organize a Gospel Crusade and get churches mobilized in unity in just a couple of weeks, all the while doing multiple youth crusades a day. It was challenging at times, but we knew the Lord was in it, so we persevered.

Evangelist Michael Job had done many crusades before, and although we learned how to plan and organize one in the Bootcamp, hands-on is something I had yet to experience. He and our other evangelist friend, Marie, had connections in Rwanda and did much of the heavy lifting of the crusade behind the scenes. I am profoundly grateful for their dedication. Preaching on the platform is the easy part. It is the ongoing work behind the scenes, usually even months before a crusade, where much of the work happens. There are so many moving parts, and every detail must be done with intentionality.

I remember my team was in the car one day talking about having the crusade. They were discussing who would preach for the four nights. We needed four evangelists to preach the Gospel and four to teach and demonstrate the healing portion. I heard the Lord say in my spirit, "Preach." I thought, "Oh no, I am not ready. I came here to do Youth Crusades." A few minutes passed, and I received a text from my Mama saying, "Are you preaching?" The Holy Ghost had woken her up and had her write that at that very moment. I thought, "Okay, Lord, I suppose you want me to preach!"

I had yet to tell my colleagues what the Lord said to me. We had been at a wedding of a close friend of one of the evangelists that were there, and I began to tell of how I would have the visions of mass crusades. Then one of the evangelist looked over and said, "Why are you not preaching at the Crusade?" And that is how the Lord opened the door to preach my first Gospel Crusade.

I went to Rwanda to join the mission of 500,000 souls of precious children being saved, and the Lord opened the door for me to preach a crusade, be on the radio to share my testimony, and be on television twice! I was in utter amazement at how the Lord was opening doors. We saw over 700,000 children receive Jesus and be filled with the Holy Ghost on that trip! Teams went over there until the end of 2022 and hit the one million mark of the harvest of souls in Rwanda! Go Jesus!

I will never forget being on that platform that day. It was a fulfillment of the visions for years the Lord showed me by the Spirit. Being able to be used to preach His glorious Gospel to the masses; to see so many healed and delivered was truly a dream come true! Since my first power encounter with the Holy Spirit, my heart has been to preach the Gospel in power and see lives transformed! 2 Timothy 3:5 says, "Having a form of godliness, but denying the power thereof: from such turn away." For years I lived in a dead religion. I was still bound, but once I encountered the power of God, I was never to be the same. I want this generation to see the Glory of God!

There was one lady in particular that I will never forget from the Gospel Crusade. She was brought to the crusade on a bike by a friend. She was paralyzed from the waist down but was healed and left that field jumping! It turns out there were two others that night that were previously paralyzed and were healed. The Lord is the healer, but I have noticed that sometimes there is a special grace for a particular healing in a meeting; in this case, the Lord chose to heal paralytics.

Looking back at the Rwanda trip, I see how the Lord opened exceeding, abundantly, above all that I could ask or imagine (Ephesians 3:20). He is the great unfolder of the plans He has for you. When you step out in obedience, watch what He will do to show Himself strong! I know in myself, I felt like I was not ready to preach a crusade, but the Lord said I was in HIM. The Lord does not call you to where you are comfortable. This is not about feeling "ready." After all the amazing training in organizing and preaching crusades, I still had these feelings but pushed past them. Get beyond yourself!

When the Lord says it is time, it is time. It is not about your ability but about His ability through you. We are just vessels, and we must not consider ourselves too much. In Exodus 4, when the Lord called Moses to be a deliverer for the Israelites,

Moses said, "They will not trust me. They will not listen to a word I say, God? Appear to him? Hardly!" He doubted in his heart his ability. If God says it, you can take it to the bank!

In my own life, I have noticed a pattern. The Lord will open opportunities to speak before His people, and I will find out soon before it happens. I believe He does this, so I will not overthink it in my head. If we keep our hearts prepared by being with Him, then there will be an ease in the flow. 2 Timothy 4 says, "Preach the Word; be prepared in season and out of season; correct, rebuke and encourage—with great patience and careful instruction." In other words, be ready by prioritizing being with Him, and when He opens the door, you will be ready.

Another testimony of this happening was recently while our Christ for all Nations teams were in Zambia, Africa, during the Decapolis Crusades. During this Decapolis, there were eleven crusades in eleven cities in Zambia, simultaneously over two weeks. We had seen over one million souls come into the Kingdom with all of the teams. It truly was a phenomenal trip!

The Bootcamp Director, Levi Lutz, had been preaching at the location where we were serving, and I remember thinking that he would ask me to help pray for the sick. It was an unction from the Holy Ghost, and I had even shared it with my mom that night. Evangelist Levi approached me the next day, asking if I wanted to help pray for the sick. It is a perfect example of staying ready and allowing the Lord to keep your heart ready to flow with whatever doors He opens.

The day I was asked to pray for the sick, I had gone to our vehicle to grab a snack from my backpack, and this little toddler ran out of nowhere. He bowed down on his knees and lifted one hand toward me. I did not understand what he was doing, and I looked over, very perplexed at our driver, who was a local in the city we were in. He told me this was a sign of respect and honor. The young man had been well-disciplined, he said. I told the boy to stand up and looked at the father to ask his name. It turns out his name was Destiny. I realized later just how prophetic this was. This little boy Destiny had bowed down to show honor, but the destiny the Lord had for me was meeting me and honoring me at this time. I love the way the Father speaks to His children so intimately.

After having the opportunity to pray for about 40,000 people, we saw many healings. Canes, chairs, and walkers all went up across the sea of people as a testament to what Jesus had done. One gentleman had been in a car accident four months prior and could not walk without crutches. After prayer, he could walk just fine, so we threw the crutches off the platform. One night we had a lady that we had prayed for at one of our local outreaches that was wheeled in a wheelbarrow and could not walk. She was at the crusade walking just fine a week later! I could share testimony after testimony, but this is the healing power of Jesus. Just as much as He died on the cross for our salvation, he also died for our healing in every part of our being!

16.

Fulfillment

Not long after I returned home from Rwanda in Spring 2022, I received a call from a friend of mine from the Bootcamp, Evangelist Eliot Morgan. He and I had been on the same squad in the last training. He was now relocated to Orlando and had become the personal assistant to Evangelist Lutz. They had been in a meeting discussing who in the area could help with scheduling and interviews for the next Bootcamp. My name had come up, and they wanted to know if I would be willing. The Holy Ghost brought to remembrance the dream I had while in

Alabama of me serving the Bootcamp. Of course, I gladly accepted!

Administration work is not something I would say that I am strong in, but it has caused me to have a greater dependence on the Lord. Let's just say that I have grown in my admin skills. What an honor to be asked to make the calls to let the applicants know they have been accepted into a training that will, hands down, change their lives forever. I still have the first voicemail on my phone saved from when CfaN first called me to let me know I had been accepted through the first phase of the application process!

With much prayer in the fear of the Lord, I began scheduling and doing interviews, and amazingly, through His grace, I was good at it. Again, the Lord is not looking for your capabilities. I am reminded of when I was in Bible College working in the local church department, and they told me I was doing phone calls for new guests to see how their experience was and to pray for them. At first, I thought, "Whoa, whoa, I don't even like being on the phone, much less with people I don't know!" Most women enjoy being on the phone, me not so much. I knew I needed the grace of God on that one, and it turns out, by His grace, I did very well in that.

It may surprise some people, but back in college, when taking public speaking, I would be so nervous speaking in front of people. For the Lord to call me to speak in front of people, in my own natural eyes, seemed crazy because, again, I know me!

The Lord does not always call you to areas in which you "feel" like you are good in. He calls you to areas you are most weak in because in our weakness, He is strong (2nd Corinthians 12:9). He alone gets the Glory in these instances because we know ourselves and how weak we truly are. Stop looking to yourself and see the limitless God that lives inside you! Stop making excuses and let Him use you for His Glory.

If you do not step out in obedience to what the Lord is asking of you, I have noticed in my own life that He has a way of causing situations to turn to get you out of a place. It is like a mother eagle pushing her eaglets out of the nest. I remember I worked at a salon where I made a salary plus tips, but I knew the Lord wanted me to go to my friend's salon that she had just opened. The only thing is that I would not make an hourly wage at my friend's salon. I would be making commissions on the clients that I received. This took faith, which is ultimately trust.

This was in the beginning years of walking with the Lord, and I did not have the faith to step out, but He pushed me out. Things started going haywire at work. The boss was acting weird toward me, and the favor that I once had with the clients changed dramatically. I had peace about going to my friend's salon, but I still reasoned about finances. The Lord gave me a little push on that one! The longer you walk with the Lord, the more you know He is good and has your best interest in mind.

After having the privilege to serve prior to the Bootcamp starting, I had the privilege of being able to serve throughout the duration of the training. Seeing the students from the beginning of the training to the Initiation trip in Africa, where they got to practice all they had learned, was astounding. There was such accelerated growth. Many of them did not even look the same outwardly, so you know that such work was done inwardly. Being able to equip and train others, and love people in their calling, is such a great honor.

There had been many years of preparation until the Bootcamp training, but I am walking in my purpose and destiny. I had felt like my whole life had been prepared for this moment. It is what I was born for!

After the Light the Fire Again Conference in the Fall of 22', I read a post on Facebook that a friend, Evangelist Evelina Smane, had written while we were heading home to Orlando. She wrote about attending a conference when she was fifteen where she met Reinhard Bonnke, and now she is serving His legacy. I thought in my heart, "Lord, I would have loved to have met Reinhard." When I arrived home, I was putting up some of Bonnke's books on my bookshelf that we had received. I heard by the Spirit, "You have been engrafted into the legacy, daughter." The wild thing is, I heard this in Reinhard's German accent! I was blown away but did not say a word about it. I entered the living room, and Mama said, "Are you happy?" Famous words of Reinhard! I still did not say a word, because I was still seeking the Lord on this. I know we are not to talk to people who have passed, but I clearly heard this with my spiritual ears!

At a prayer meeting at the Christ for all Nations Ministry Center the next day, someone mentioned the great cloud of witnesses in Hebrews 12. After we left the meeting, my Mama said my sister Laurie said, "There is a cloud in here." My Mama thought she said, "Reinhard is in here!" At that moment, I knew Reinhard was in the great cloud of witnesses, and I had indeed heard him by the Spirit!

We, as Holy Spirit evangelists, have been given the torch to win a generation to the saving knowledge of Jesus. I hope this book gives you some hope, knowing that Jesus is HOPE and He has an amazing, adventurous plan for you. Do not sit on the sidelines, watching those around you fulfill the call of God on their lives. It does not matter what you have done or where you have come from, He still wants to use you! For years I felt that I could never amount to anything, and that was a lie from the pit of hell!

You are created for BIG things; the Lord will restore all the devil has stolen from you. The Lord wants to use the scars of the past as a testament of what He has brought you through! SOAR, child of God, the time is NOW to fulfill all the Father has for you. Every hurt and every bit of pain can be used for His Glory. There are souls connected to your yes. Do not delay but obey!

If you have never repented of your sins and made Jesus Lord of your Life, you can say this prayer with your heart open:

Dear Lord Jesus,

I ask you to forgive me of my sins,

I ask you to come into my heart,

I ask you to be Lord of my life.

I turn away from sin.

And turn to you, Jesus,

Wash me with your Blood,

And make me new.

Fill me with your Holy Spirit,

And help me to live for You.

In Jesus' name,

Amen.

STAY CONNECTED

If you have just received salvation, you are now a child of God! All of Heaven is rejoicing. I encourage you to get plugged into a local church, get water baptized, and walk this journey of life with King Jesus. God bless you, abundantly!

If you would like to share a testimony of how the Lord has blessed you through the reading of this book, I would love to hear from you:
Email- Yourpainisnotinvain1@gmail.com
Facebook- Jennifer Elizabeth Whitaker
Instagram- Kingdom_comeministries
Website- kingdomcomeministries.us

Made in the USA
Columbia, SC
28 June 2024

37731220R00117